Thermo-Dynamic Thrills

Written by Wallie Winholtz
Kathy Cramer & Sherry Twyman
Illustrations and humorous asides,
B. K. Hixson

Thermo-Dynamic Thrills

Copyright © 2002
First Printing • July 2002
B. K. Hixson

Published by Loose in the Lab, Inc.
9462 South 560 West
Sandy, Utah 84070

www.looseinthelab.com

Library of Congress Cataloging-in-Publication Data:

Hixson, B. K.
 Thermodynamic Thrills/B. K. Hixson
 p.   cm.-(Loose in the Lab Science Series)

 Includes index
 ISBN 0-9660965-2-8
 1. Heat experiments-juvenile literature. [1. Heat
experiments 2. Experiments] I. B. K. Hixson II. Loose in
the Lab III. Title IV. Series
QP441.D54   2002
152.14

Printed in the United States of America
Some like it hot!

The Authors

Kathy, Wallie & Sherry

All three hail from the heartland of America where they nurture and guide the youth of America, crafting the next generation of scientists, engineers, politicians, artists, and vagrant boxcar inhabitants in search of the next great American novel.

Just for the record we, at Loose in the Lab, are doing the dedicating of this book to them. They are simply unsuspecting victims of our appreciations.

Dick Roeter, PhD.

Thank you for making physics something that all of your students could not only understand but embrace and enjoy. This dedication is slightly off center in honor of your style of presentation.

Acknowledgments

Getting a book out for public consumption is far from a one-man job. There are lots of thank-yous to be doodled out and at the risk of leaving someone out, we attempt to do that on this page. In terms of my physics education, that didn't really begin in earnest until my freshman year of college under the tutelage of Dick Roeter. He had a rather unorthodox way of introducing the world of thermodynamics to us, and I am forever appreciative of his interest in our acquisition of the ideas through hands-on experimentation rather than exhausting us with countless equations, proofs, and exercises—all orbiting an abstract world that never really allows you to grasp the idea fully.

As for my educational outlook, the hands-on perspective, and the use of humor in the classroom, Dr. Fox, my senior professor at Oregon State University, gets the credit for shaping my educational philosophy while simultaneously recognizing that even at the collegiate level we were on to something a little different. He did his very best to encourage, nurture, and support me while I was getting basket loads of opposition for being willing to swim upstream. There were also several colleagues who helped to channel my enthusiasm during those early, formative years of teaching: Dick Bishop, Dick Hinton, Dee Strange, Connie Ridgway, and Linda Zimmermann. Thanks for your patience, friendship, and support.

Next up are all the folks that get to do the dirty work that make the final publication look so polished but very rarely get the credit they deserve. Our resident graphics guru Kris Barton gets a nod for scanning and cleaning the artwork you find on these pages, as well as putting together the graphics that make up the cover. A warm Yankee yahoo to Sue Moore our editor who passes her comments on so that Kathleen Hixson, and Sue Moore (once again) can take turns simultaneously proofreading the text while mocking my writing skills.

Once we have a finished product, it has to be printed by the good folks at Excel Graphics—Kurt Walker, Kris and the crew—so that Louisa Walker, Kent Walker, Tracy St. Pierre, and the Delta Education gang can market and ship the books, collect the money, and send us a couple of nickels. It's a short thank-you for a couple of very important jobs.

Mom and Dad, as always, get the end credits. Thanks for the education, encouragement, and love. And for Kathy and the kids—Porter, Shelby, Courtney, and Aubrey—hugs and kisses.

Repro Rights

There is very little about this book that is truly formal, but at the insistence of our wise and esteemed counsel, let us declare: *No part of this book may be reproduced or utilized in any form or by any means, electronic or mechanical, including photocopying, recording, or by any information storage and retrieval system, without permission in writing from the publisher.* That would be us.

More Legal Stuff

Official disclaimer for you aspiring scientists and lab groupies. This is a hands-on science book. By the very intent of the design, you will be directed to use common, nontoxic, household items in a safe and responsible manner to avoid injury to yourself and others who are present while you are pursuing your quest for knowledge and enlightenment in the world of physics. Just make sure that you have a fire blanket handy and a wall-mounted video camera to corroborate your story.

If, for some reason, perhaps even beyond your own control, you have an affinity for disaster, we wish you well. *But we, in no way take any responsibility for any injury that is incurred to any person using the information provided in this book or for any damage to personal property or effects that are directly or indirectly a result of the suggested activities contained herein.* Translation: You're on your own, despite the fact that many have preceded you in the lab remember that, as far the brain is concerned, there is very little difference between frostbite and 4000 degrees Fahrenheit. It will remind you of your poor decision no matter which direction you go.

Less Formal Legal Stuff

If you happen to be a home-schooler or very enthusiastic school teacher please feel free to make copies of this book for your classroom or personal family use—one copy per student, up to 35 students. If you would like to use an experiment from this book for a presentation to your faculty or school district, we would be happy to oblige. Just give us a whistle and we will send you a release for the particular lab activity you wish to use. Please contact us at the address below. Thanks.

Special Requests
Loose in the Lab, Inc.
9462 South 560 West
Sandy, Utah 84070

Table of Contents

National Content Standards • Grades 5–8
C. Heat

Heat can be produced in many ways, such as burning, rubbing, or mixing one substance with another. Heat can move from one object to another by conduction.

The 14 Big Ideas About Heat & Corresponding Labs

Idea 1. Heat is a form of energy and can be produced by friction between two objects, electricity flowing through an object, light being absorbed by an object, or combining one chemical substance with another.

Idea 2. The temperature of an object is defined as the average amount of heat and is measured using a tool called a thermometer. Temperature is independent of the mass of an object.

Idea 3. When the temperature of a material increases, the motion of the atoms in that material also increases. When the temperature decreases, the speed of the molecules also decreases.

Idea 4. Heat is measured in units called calories. The more mass an object has the more heat it can store. The amount of heat an object can absorb is measured as its specific heat.

Idea 5. Heat always moves from hot to cold. The greater the difference in temperature between two objects, the faster their temperatures change.

Idea 6. Insulation is the ability of a material to prevent the movement of heat.

Even More Contents

Idea 7. Heat waves can radiate through a vacuum or gas in all directions. Gases expand when they are heated and contract when they are cooled.

Idea 8. Heat can travel through gases and liquids as a convection current. Liquids and gases expand when they are heated and contract when they are cooled.

Idea 9. Heat can be conducted through solids. Solids expand when they are heated and contract when they are cooled. The amount that they change is measured as the coefficient of expansion.

Idea 10. Added heat can cause solids to change state and become liquids. This is called the melting point of a substance and it is used to identify the material. Added heat can also cause liquids to change state and become gases. This is called the boiling point of a substance and it is used to identify the material.

Idea 11. If enough heat is added to a material that it bursts into flames, it has reached a temperature called the kindling point.

Idea 12. Removing heat can cause gases to change state and become liquids. This is called the condensation point of a substance and it is used to identify the material. Removing heat can also cause liquids to change state and become solids. This is called the freezing point of a substance and it is used to identify the material.

Idea 13. Some materials change directly from solids to gases or from gases to solids. This characteristic is called sublimation.

Idea 14. Heat causes the molecules in some substances to rearrange. When this happens, a measurable change can be observed.

Who Are You ? And . . .

First of all, we may have an emergency at hand and we'll both want to cut to the chase and get the patient into the cardiac unit if necessary. So, before we go too much further, **define yourself**. Please check one and only one choice listed below and then immediately follow the directions that follow *in italics*. Thank you in advance for your cooperation.

I am holding this book because …

___ **A. I am a responsible, but panicked, parent.** My son / daughter / triplets (circle one) just informed me that his / her / their science fair project is due tomorrow. This is the only therapy I could afford on such short notice. Which means that if I was not holding this book, my hands would be encircling the soon-to-be-worm-bait's neck.

Directions: Can't say this is the first or the last time we heard that one. Hang in there, we can do this.

1. Quickly read the Table of Contents with the worm bait. The Big Ideas define what each section is about. Obviously, the kid is not passionate about science, or you would not be in this situation. See if you can find an idea that causes some portion of an eyelid or facial muscle to twitch.

If that does not work, we recommend narrowing the list to the following labs because they are fast, use materials that can be acquired with limited notice, and the intrinsic level of interest is generally quite high.

How to Use This Book

2. Take the materials list from the lab write-up and from page 205 of the Science Fair Project section and go shopping.

3. Assemble the materials and perform the lab at least once. Gather as much data as you can.

4. Go to page 182 and read the material. Then start on Step 1 of Preparing Your Science Fair Project. With any luck you can dodge an academic disaster.

___ **B. I am worm bait.** My science fair project is due tomorrow, and there is not anything moldy in the fridge. I need a big Band-Aid, in a hurry.

Directions: Same as Option A. You can decide if and when you want to clue your folks in on your current dilemma.

___ **C. I am the parent of a student who informed me that he/ she has been assigned a science fair project due in six to eight weeks.** My son/daughter has expressed an interest in science books with humorous illustrations that attempt to explain heat and associated phenomena.

Who Are You ? And . . .

Directions: Well, you came to the right place. Give your kid these directions and stand back.

1. The first step is to read through the Table of Contents and see if anything grabs your interest. Read through several experiments, see if the science teacher has any of the more difficult materials to acquire like bimetallic strips, convection rods, conduction wheels, radiometers, and ask if they can be borrowed. Play with the experiments and see which one really tickles your fancy.

2. After you have found and conducted an experiment that you like, take a peek at the Science Fair Ideas and see if you would like to investigate one of those or create an idea of your own. The guidelines for those are listed in the Science Fair section. You have plenty of time so you can fiddle and fool with the original experiment and its derivations several times. Work until you have an original question you want to answer and then start the process. You are well on your way to an excellent grade.

___ D. I am a responsible student and have been assigned a science fair project due in six to eight weeks. I am interested in heat, and despite demonstrating maturity and wisdom well beyond the scope of my peers, I too still have a sense of humor. Enlighten and entertain me.

Directions: Cool. Being teachers, we have heard reports of this kind of thing happening but usually in an obscure and hard-to-locate town several states removed. Nonetheless, congratulations.

Same as Option C. You have plenty of time and should be able to score very well. We'll keep our eyes peeled when the Nobel Prizes are announced in a couple of decades.

How to Use This Book

___ **E. I am a parent who home schools my child/children.** We are always on the lookout for quality curriculum materials that are not only educationally sound but also kid- and teacher-friendly. I am not particularly strong in science, but I realize it is a very important topic. How is this book going to help me out?

Directions: In a lot of ways we created this book specifically for home schoolers.

1. We have taken the National Content Standards, the guidelines that are used by all public and private schools nationwide to establish their curriculum base, and listed them in the Table of Contents. You now know where you stand with respect to the national standards.

2. We then break these standards down and list the major ideas that you should want your kid to know. We call these the Big Ideas. Some people call them objectives, others call them curriculum standards, educational benchmarks, or assessment norms. Same apple, different name. The bottom line is that when your child is done studying this unit on heat you want him or her not only to understand and explain each of the fourteen Big Ideas listed in this book, but also, to be able to defend and argue their position based on experiential evidence that they have collected.

3. Building on the Big Ideas, we have collected and rewritten 50 hands-on science labs. Each one has been specifically selected so that it supports the Big Idea that it is correlated to. This is critical. As the kids do the science experiment, they see, smell, touch, and hear the experiment. They will store that information in several places in their brains. When it comes time to comprehend the Big Idea, the concrete hands-on experiences provide the foundation for building the Idea, which is quite often abstract. Kids who merely read about temperature scales, conduction, convection, and radiation, or who see pictures of convection currents or thermal couples but have never measured or felt their effect are trying to build abstract ideas on abstract ideas and quite often miss the mark.

Who Are You ? And . . .

For example: I can show you a recipe in a book for chocolate chip cookies and ask you to reiterate it. Or I can turn you loose in a kitchen, have you mix the ingredients, grease the pan, plop the dough on the cookie sheet, slide everything into the oven, and wait impatiently until they pop out eight minutes later. Chances are that the description given by the person who actually made the cookies is going to be much clearer because it is based on their true understanding of the process, **because it is based on experience.**

4. Once you have completed the experiment, there are a number of extension ideas under the Science Fair Extensions that allow you to spend as much or as little time on the ideas as you deem necessary.

5. A word about humor. Science is not usually known for being funny even though Bill Nye, The Science Guy, *Beaker from* Sesame Street, *and* Beakman's World *do their best to mingle the two. That's all fine and dandy, but we want you to know that we incorporate humor because it is scientifically (and educationally) sound to do so. Plus it's really at the root of our personalities. Here's what we know:*

When we laugh . . .
a. Our pupils dilate, increasing the amount of light entering the eye.
b. Our heart rate increases, which pumps more blood to the brain.
c. Oxygen-rich blood to the brain means the brain is able to collect, process, and store more information. Big I.E.: increased comprehension.
d. Laughter relaxes muscles, which can be involuntarily tense if a student is uncomfortable or fearful of an academic topic.
e. Laughter stimulates the immune system, which will ultimately translate into overall health and fewer kids who say they are sick of science.
f. Socially, it provides an acceptable pause in the academic routine, which then gives the student time to regroup and prepare to address some of the more difficult ideas with a renewed spirit. They can study longer and focus on ideas more efficiently.
g. Laughter releases chemicals in the brain that are associated with pleasure and joy.
6. If you follow the book in the order it is written, you will be able to build ideas and concepts in a logical and sequential pattern. But that is by no means necessary. For a complete set of guidelines on our ideas on how to teach home-schooled kids science, check out our book, Why's the Cat on Fire? How to Excel at Teaching Science to Your Home-Schooled Kids.

How to Use This Book

___ F. **I am a public/private school teacher,** and this looks like an interesting book to add ideas to my classroom lesson plans.

Directions: It is, and please feel free to do so. However, while this is a great classroom resource for kids, may we also recommend several other titles: Can't Touch That *(basic intro to heat),* That's the Point *(temperature scales and solids, liquids, and gases),* CCR: Conduction, Convection, and Radiation *(movement of heat).*

These books have teacher-preparation pages, student-response sheets or lab pages, lesson plans, bulletin board ideas, discovery center ideas, vocabulary sheets, unit pretests, unit exams, lab practical exams, and student grading sheets. Basically everything you need if you are a science nincompoop, and a couple of cool ideas if you are a seasoned veteran with an established curriculum. All of the ideas that are covered in this one book are covered much more thoroughly in the other two. They were specifically written for teachers.

___ G. **My son/daughter/grandson/niece/father-in-law** is interested in science, and this looks like fun.

Directions: Congratulations on your selection. Add a gift certificate to the local science supply store and a package of hot chocolate mix and you have the perfect rainy Saturday afternoon gig.

___ H. **My cooking class is concerned about the decomposition of fatty acids in a high pH environment, in particular, with respect to the role of bonding sites relative to temperature sensitivity. Can you help?**

Directions: Nope. Try the Sous Chef down the street.

Lab Safety

Contained herein are 50 science activities to help you better understand the nature and characteristics of heat as we currently understand these things. However, since you are on your own in this journey we thought it prudent to share some basic wisdom and experience in the safety department.

Read the Instructions

An interesting concept, especially if you are a teenager. Take a minute before you jump in and get going to read all of the instructions as well as warnings. If you do not understand something, stop and ask an adult for help.

Clean Up All Messes

Keep your lab area clean. It will make it easier to put everything away at the end and may also prevent contamination and the subsequent germination of a species of mutant tomato bug larva. You will also find that chemicals perform with more predictability if they are not poisoned with foreign molecules.

Organize

Translation: Put it back where you get it. If you need any more clarification, there is an opening at the landfill for you.

Dispose of Poisons Properly

This will not be much of a problem with the labs that are suggested in this book. However, if you happen to wander over into one of the many disciplines that incorporates the use of more advanced chemicals, then we would suggest that you use great caution with the materials and definitely dispose of any and all poisons properly.

Practice Good Fire Safety

If there is a fire in the room, notify an adult immediately. If an adult is not in the room and the fire is manageable, smother the outbreak with a fire blanket or use a fire extinguisher. When the fire is contained, immediately send someone to find an adult. If, for any reason, you happen to catch on fire, **REMEMBER: Stop, Drop, and Roll.** Never run; it adds oxygen to the fire, making it burn faster, and it also scares the bat guano out of the neighbors when they see the neighbor kids running down the block doing an imitation of a campfire marshmallow without the stick.

Protect Your Skin

It is a good idea to always wear protective gloves whenever you are working with chemicals. Again, this particular book does not suggest or incorporate hazardous chemicals in its lab activities. This is because we are primarily incorporating only safe, manageable kinds of chemicals for these labs. If you do happen to spill a chemical on your skin, notify an adult immediately and then flush the area with water for 15 minutes. It's unlikely, but if irritation develops, have your parents or another responsible adult look at it. If it appears to be of concern, contact a physician. Take any information that you have about the chemical with you.

Lab Safety

Save Your Nose Hairs

Sounds like a cause celebre L.A. style, but it is really good advice. To smell a chemical to identify it, hold the open container six to ten inches down and away from your nose. Make a clockwise circular motion with your hand over the opening of the container, "wafting" some of the fumes toward your nose. This will allow you to safely smell some of the fumes without exposing youself to a large dose of anything noxious. This technique may help prevent a nosebleed or your lungs from accidentally getting burned by chemicals.

Wear Goggles If Appropriate

If the lab asks you to heat or mix chemicals, be sure to wear protective eyewear. Also have an eyewash station or running water available. You never know when something is going to splatter, splash, or react unexpectedly. It is better to look like a nerd and be prepared than schedule a trip down to pick out a Seeing Eye dog. If you do happen to accidentally get chemicals in your eye, flush the area for 15 minutes. If any irritation or pain develops, immediately go see a doctor.

Lose the Comedy Routine

You should have plenty of time scheduled during your day to mess around, but science lab is not one of them. Horseplay breaks glassware, spills chemicals, and creates unnecessary messes—things that parents do not appreciate. Trust us on this one.

No Eating

Do not eat while performing a lab. Putting your food in the lab area contaminates your food and the experiment. This makes for bad science and worse indigestion. Avoid poisoning yourself and goobering up your lab ware by observing this rule.

Happy and safe experimenting!

Recommended Materials Suppliers

For every lesson in this book we offer a list of materials. Many of these are very easy to acquire, and if you do not have them in your home already, you will be able to find them at the local grocery or hardware store. For more difficult items we have selected, for your convenience, a small but respectable list of suppliers who will meet your needs in a timely and economical manner. Call for a catalog or quote on the item that you are looking for, and they will be happy to give you a hand.

Loose in the Lab
9462 South 560 West
Sandy, Utah 84070
Phone 1-888-403-1189
Fax 1-801-568-9586
www.looseinthelab.com

Delta Education
80 NW Boulevard
Nashua, NH 03601
Phone 1-800-442-5444
Fax 1-800-282-9560
www.delta-education.com

Nasco
901 Jonesville Ave.
Fort Atkinson, Wisconsin 53538
Phone 1-414-563-2446
Fax 1-920-563-8296
www.nascofa.com

Ward's Scientific
5100 W Henrietta Road
Rochester, New York 14692
Phone 800-387-7822
Fax 1-716-334-6174
www.wardsci.com

Educational Innovations
362 Main Avenue
Norwalk, Conneticut 06851
Phone 1-888-912-7474
Fax 1-203-229-0740
www.teachersource.com

Frey Scientific
100 Paragon Parkway
Mansfield, Ohio 44903
Phone 1-800-225-FREY
Fax 1-419-589-1546
www.freyscientific.com

Fisher Scientific
485 S. Frontage Rd.
Burr Ridge, Il 60521
Phone 800-955-1177
Fax 1-800-955-0740
www.fisheredu.com

Flinn Scientific
PO Box 219
Batavia, Il. 60510
Phone 1-800 452-1261
Fax 1-630-879-6962
www.flinnsci.com

The Ideas, Lab Activities, & Science Fair Extensions

Big Idea 1

Heat is a form of energy and can be produced by friction between two objects, electricity flowing through an object, infrared waves being absorbed by an object, or combining one chemical substance with another.

What's the Rub?

The Experiment

Kinetic heat is heat that is produced when two objects are rubbed together. The contact between these objects has a degree of resistance called friction. The amount of friction determines the amount of heat that is produced—the more friction, the more heat.

In this lab the rubbing, which produces the friction, is going to be done with two hands, a pile of metal molecules trapped inside a wire, a plastic-can holder, and a hammer and nail. Welcome to the study of heat and kindly proceed.

Materials

1   Pair of hands
1   Thermometer, student, alcohol
1   Copper wire, 12-14 gauge
1   Hammer
1   Nail, #12-#16
1   Plastic six-pack holder
1   Clock with a sweep-second hand.

Procedure

1. The first experiment is one that you have performed on cold mornings for years, even if you are still an anklebiter. Using the illustration to the upper left as a guide, hold the thermometer between the palms of your hands for 30 seconds. Record the temperature in the space provided on page 24.

2. Set the thermometer on the table and rub your hands together for another 30 seconds, pressing as hard as you can.

3. Immediately replace the thermometer and record the temperature a second time.

4. Pick up the copper wire and bend it to a 45-degree angle. Place your thumb and forefinger on the bend and record the temperature that you feel.

5. Bend the wire back and forth 25 times or until it breaks. Place your thumb and forefinger on the bend and record the temperature that you feel after the wire has been bent.

6. Pick up a nail and record the temperature. Place the same nail on a hard surface and give it four or five good whacks near the pointed end. Record the temperature of the nail after it has been struck by the hammer.

7. Finally, pick up the plastic six-pack holder and record the temperature. Give it several quick stretches and record the temperature a second time.

What's the Rub?

Data & Observations

Record the temperature or circle the word that best describes the temperature for each of the following lab tests.

1. Rubbing hands

    A. Before rubbing: _____ °C

    B. After rubbing: _____ °C

2. Bending wire

    A. Before bending: **cool** or **warm**

    B. After bending: **cool** or **warm**

3. Smacking nails

    A. Before smacking: **cool** or **warm**

    B. After smacking: **cool** or **warm**

4. Plastic six-pack holder

    A. Before stretching: **cool** or **warm**

    B. After stretching: **cool** or **warm**

How Come, Huh?

1. *Why did my hands feel warmer when I rubbed them together?*

Two surfaces being rubbed together or across one another will create a transfer of mechanical energy into heat energy. When hands are rubbed together quickly, you are converting that pizza you had for lunch from chemical energy into mechanical (muscle) energy and finally into heat energy. Remember, *energy cannot be created or destroyed, only converted from one form to another.*

2. *Why does bending the wire create heat?*

As the wire is bent back and forth, the molecules rub on each other much like when you rubbed your hands together. This friction results in heat whether it be between the molecules of wire or two hands rubbing together like mad.

3. *Why does smacking the nail create heat?*

The smack brings great pressure to the area of the nail being struck, exciting the molecules. This movement creates heat, as mentioned above.

4. *Why does plastic feel warm when it is pulled apart?*

The molecules of plastic are trying desperately to hold together. Pulling in opposite directions on the plastic causes friction and thus produces heat. You can get the same results by stretching a rubber band many times and then feeling the stretched part. All that excitement creates heat as the molecules are made crazy.

Science Fair Extensions

1. Don't stop now, there are all kinds of ways to demonstrate how kinetic energy can be converted to thermal energy, or heat. Make a list of 10 sets of objects that produce heat when they come in contact with one another and produce friction.

2. List 5 other objects, besides copper wire, that produce heat when they are bent.

3. Experiment with rubber bands, elastic bands, plastic bags, and other objects that stretch and see if you can replicate the results that you found with the plastic six-pack holder.

Radiometer Studies

The Experiment

This particular lab demonstrates that visible light and infrared energy, both part of the electromagnetic spectrum, can be absorbed by a vane trapped in a glass bulb. The vane then releases the trapped energy and uses that process to cause the vane to spin.

If you are following these ideas closely, you will recognize that you are going to use light and heat energy to produce motion, the reverse of the previous lab. Again, *energy cannot be created or destroyed, simply converted from one form to another.*

Materials

1   Radiometer
1   Dark closet
1   Sunny day
1   Lamp
1   Table
1   Tall glass cylinder
    Water

Procedure

1. Place the radiometer on a level surface in a dark closet or cupboard where there is *little or no* sunlight. Look at the vanes inside the radiometer and estimate how fast they are spinning. Record your observation in the first Data section on page 28. Place your hand in front of the bulb and record how much heat you felt. Record this information in the second data table on page 28.

2. Place the radiometer on a level surface that has some *indirect sunlight* and estimate and record the speed of the vanes. Place your hand in front of the bulb and record how much heat you felt. Record this information in the other data table on page 28.

3. Place the radiometer on a level surface in *bright sunlight*. Estimate how fast the vanes are spinning. Record your observation in the space on page 28. Place your hand between the sun and the radiometer and estimate the amount of heat your felt striking the radiometer. Record this information on page 28.

4. Place a bright lamp on a table and hold the radiometer near the lamp. Observe and record the speed that the vanes are spinning when the radiometer is exposed directly to light from a lamp. Place your hand between the lamp and the radiometer and estimate the amount of heat you felt.

5. Now, place a tall cylinder of water between the lamp and the radiometer so that all the light striking the radiometer must pass through the cylinder of water first. Use the illustration below as a guide. (Vases work well; those spaghetti holders you get at cooking stores work OK too.) Record the speed that the vanes spin using this setup. One last time, place your hand between the cylinder of water and the radiometer and estimate the amount of heat you felt.

LAMP   VASE   RADIOMETER
          W/WATER

Radiometer Studies

Data & Observations

As you complete each instruction, put a check mark in the column that best describes the speed that the vanes inside the radiometer were spinning.

Amount of Direct Light

Instruction	No Motion	Moderate	Fast	Very Fast
1				
2				
3				
4				
5				

Amount of Detectable Heat

Instruction	None	Some	Burnin', Baby
1			
2			
3			
4			
5			

How Come, Huh?

Radiometers can be used to detect two kinds of electromagnetic radiation (energy)—visible light that we see and infrared light that we feel as heat.

When infrared light strikes the vanes inside the radiometer, they reflect off the silvered side of the vane. But, when they strike the black side, they are absorbed and converted to heat energy. This heat then escapes from the black side of the vane, expanding the air inside the radiometer causing a small push against the black side of the vane. Bombard the radiometer with infrared light, and the vane spins pretty fast.

The heat part of this experiment is born out in instructions 4 and 5. Lamps produce infrared heat waves. To know this all you have to do is put your hand near a bulb. Water is very good about filtering out (absorbing) those heat waves when light passes through it. By placing a cylinder of water between the lamp and the radiometer, you should have noticed a significant decrease in the speed of the vanes.

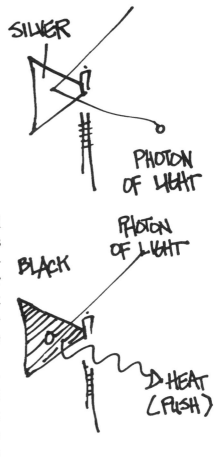

Science Fair Extensions

4. See if other liquids absorb infrared light. Try cooking oil, vinegar, rubbing alcohol, and anything else your parents give the thumbs up to.

5. Locate other sources of infrared light (an electric stove comes to mind) and see if the radiometer can detect those waves—after you get your parents permission, of course.

Nichrome Heater

The Experiment

Nichrome wire gets its name because it is an alloy—a metal formed when two pure metals are combined. In this case the two metals are nickel and chromium, making nichrome.

Nichrome wire has some unique characteristics. One of them in particular is the fact that when an electric current passes through the wire it not only gets hot, but it also glows and produces light. You will compare a nichrome wire with a piece of pure copper wire and see and feel the difference.

Materials

1   8-inch Length of nichrome wire, 00 gauge
1   8-inch Length of copper wire, 00 gauge
1   Pencil
1   D cell battery with clip
2   Alligator clips
1   6-volt Lantern battery
1   Washcloth
1   9-oz. Cup of water

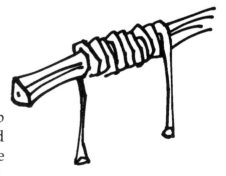

Procedure

1. Before you begin the lab you will want to take the pencil and wrap each of the wires around the shaft forming a short, loose coil. Leave about 3 inches on each end. Use the illustration above as a guide.

2. Snap the D battery into the clip. You will find two small metal tabs on either end of the clip. This is where you will attach the alligator clips.

3. Start with the copper wire. Touch the coil with your fingers and record your observations in the space provided in the section on page 32.

4. Hook the ends of the copper wire into the metal tabs and let the electricity flow for 15 seconds. Unhook the wire using the washcloth to protect your fingers and gently touch the coil.

BE VERY CAREFUL, THE WIRE GETS HOT AND MAY CAUSE A MILD BURN. You may want to wet your fingers with a little bit of water before you touch the wire.

5. Repeat the experiment using the nichrome wire loop. Record your observations in the space provided on the next page. Use caution when unhooking the wire.

6. Repeat the experiment using the lantern battery and the two wire loops. Record your observations in the spaces provided on the next page. Use caution when unhooking the wires especially with the 6-volt battery. There is a lot more electricity flowing through the wires the second time.

Nichrome Heater

Data & Observations

Circle the word that best describes the temperature of the wire for each of the following lab tests.

1. Copper wire & D Battery

   A. Before electricity: **cool**, **warm**, **hot**, **very hot**

   B. After electricity: **cool**, **warm**, **hot**, **very hot**

2. Nichrome wire & D Battery

   A. Before electricity: **cool**, **warm**, **hot**, **very hot**

   B. After electricity: **cool**, **warm**, **hot**, **very hot**

3. Copper wire & Lantern Battery

   A. Before electricity: **cool**, **warm**, **hot**, **very hot**

   B. After electricity: **cool**, **warm**, **hot**, **very hot**

4. Nichrome wire & Lantern Battery

   A. Before electricity: **cool**, **warm**, **hot**, **very hot**

   B. After electricity: **cool**, **warm**, **hot**, **very hot**

How Come, Huh?

The nichrome wire has a relatively high resistance, electrically speaking, compared to the copper wire. What this means is that as the electrons go zipping through the wire they do not have a clear pathway to travel. Instead they bump into the metal atoms in the wire. Each time they do, they lose a little bit of energy, and all those little bits of energy add up to a lot of heat quickly.

Imagine you are walking down a hallway to the bathroom and you are in a hurry. If the hallway is clear of other students, you can make your way from your room to the commode in short order and without any distractions. There is little resistance to your movement.

Now, let's say you still have to go to the bathroom, but the hallway is crammed with kids on their way to lunch. You try to go as fast as you did the first time, but you keep running into folks, having to dodge people, and expend a lot of energy to get to the same place. In other words there is a lot of resistance to your movement. Same thing in the wires, only the electrons are not as polite as you are, and they bump into metal atoms as they go; and like the very first experiment in the book, you know that produces heat.

Science Fair Extensions

6. Experiment with different gauges or thicknesses of nichrome or copper wire. See if the diameter of the wire affects the temperature of the wire. Do not change the amount of electricity—just the diameter of the wire.

7. OK, now its time to change the amount of electricity. Hook batteries up to the wire and record the amount of time it takes for the wire to reach a certain temperature. Hook two batteries up in series and then three.

Hand Warmer

The Experiment

Chemicals are made up of atoms hooked together forming groups called molecules. In some cases the chemical energy that holds these atoms together can be released as heat energy. Another in our continuing series of our "See, we told you, *energy cannot be created or destroyed, it is just converted from one form to another*" labs.

In this particular lab you will add a chemical that is used to melt snow off sidewalks to water. When the chemical dissolves and the molecules break apart, you will notice a significant difference in the temperature of the water.

Materials

1   Resealable baggie
   Water
1   Quarter-cup measuring cup
1   Thermometer, student, alcohol
1   Bottle of calcium chloride pellets

Procedure

1. Fill the baggie half full, approximately 6 to 8 ounces, with room-temperature tap water. Insert the thermometer and record the temperature in the space provided on the next page.

2. Open the bottle of calcium chloride and add a quarter of a cup of pellets to the baggie. Zip the baggie closed and tip it back and forth several times, dissolving the calcium chloride into the solution. You should notice a distinct temperature increase.

3. Insert the thermometer in the water and record the temperature a second time.

Data & Observations

Record the temperature of the water for each of the following lab tests.

1. Tap water: _____ °C

2. Tap water with calcium chloride: _____ °C

How Come, Huh?

When calcium chloride is mixed in water, it splits apart forming calcium and chloride ions. When this happened, the energy that was holding the molecule together was released as heat.

Science Fair Extensions

8. Experiment to find out if the beginning temperature of the water affects the speed of the reaction.

9. Another common chemical reaction is pepper on the tongue. Find out what a Scoville unit is and why some peppers are so hot.

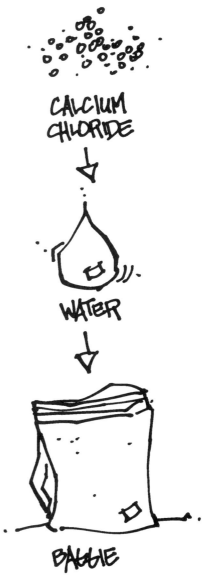

CALCIUM CHLORIDE

WATER

BAGGIE

Big Idea 2

The temperature of an object is defined as the average amount of heat and is measured using a tool called a thermometer. Temperature is independent of the mass of an object.

Fingermometers

The Experiment

Scientists use a tool called a thermometer to measure temperature. In fact, the name gives away the function. *Therm* translates to "heat," and a *meter* is "a unit of measure." So, a *thermometer* would be a tool that measures heat.

This lab will demonstrate why tools are more reliable when recording temperature than human fingers, also known as your digits—hence the title of the lab.

Materials

3 #303 Soup cans, empty
1 Celsius/ Fahrenheit thermometer
1 Pair of hands
1 Clock with sweep-second hand
   Hot water
   Cold water
   Ice cubes (optional)
   Room-temperature water

Procedure

1. Place the 3 soup cans in front of you on the table. Each can should have the top removed and be clean inside. You can snack when the lab is over.

2. Fill the first can on the right with hot water from the tap. The second can, on the left, should have very cold water from the tap and even a couple of ice cubes if you can swing it. The third can, between the other two, should be full of room-temperature water.

Fingermometers

3. Wrap your right hand around the can with the hot water and your left hand around the can with the ice cold water. Leave your hands wrapped around the cans for exactly one minute.

4. When one minute is up, remove both hands and place them both on the middle can at the same time, holding opposite sides. Use the illustrations to the right as a guide.

Record the temperature that you feel with each hand in the space provided on the next page.

5. Reverse the process. Switch cans with the hands and hold the hot can in your left hand and the cold can in your right hand. Keep them there for one minute each and then place both hands on the middle can.

Compare the results of this experiment with the results of the first experiment. Determine if your hands respond the same or if your right hand is different from your left.

6. When you are done, you can empty the water down the drain and dry out the cans.

Data & Observations

1. Circle the choice written below in bold that best describes what you felt with each hand as you touched the middle can.

    a. The temperature of the middle can felt **warmer, cooler,** or the **same** as the can full of *hot* water when I touched it with my *right* hand.

    b. The temperature of the middle can felt **warmer, cooler,** or the **same** as the can full of *cold* water when I touched it with my *left* hand.

2. Describe what you felt when you had both hands on the middle can. _____

_____

_____

3. Why would hands be considered poor instruments for recording temperature? _____

_____

_____

4. Record the actual temperature reading for each can in spaces provided.

Can	Celsius	Fahrenheit
Hot		
Middle		
Cold		

Fingermometers

How Come, Huh?

When you place your hand in cold water, it immediately starts to adapt. It closes down the size of the cells on the surface of the skin so that heat loss is minimized, coordination is reduced, and your hand becomes less flexible. When you place your hand around the warm can, the circulation in your fingers increases, muscles relax, and flexibility increases. When you grab the middle can, your hands are confused about this new addition to the family.

The hand that was cold now feels a relatively warm can. The hand that was hot now feels a relatively cool can—two hands, one person, two ideas. That's why we need the thermometer to provide an unbiased, objective measurement.

Science Fair Extensions

10. You can repeat the experiment and instead of holding the outside of the cans you can take two different metals, copper and aluminum for example, and then place them on a piece of plastic that is in the middle. You'll have to do some research to find out how this kind of conduction works in the human body.

11. Research why water boils at different temperatures depending on the altitude.

12. Why doesn't salt water freeze at 32 degrees F?

13. Skin has cool receptors and warm receptors but not "burning" receptors. The sense of burning hot is actually created by three receptors firing together—pain, cool, and warmth.

Create an alternating grid of warm and cool metal bars for the fingers on your hand, and your brain will scream "too hot to touch" when you place your hand on these bars.

Thermometer Rules!

The Experiment

Fingers are nice to have, but as you saw in the previous experiment, they aren't very reliable as thermometers. There are also safety concerns—who wants to stick their finger in a pot of boiling water to see if the temperature is just right? Thermometers were invented to measure the amount of heat in an object.

This lab will introduce you to two of the three temperatures scales used in the world today. You will learn how to read the thermometers and record the temperatures accurately.

Materials

1   1000-ml Beaker or quart saucepan
    Ice cubes
    Water
1   C° Thermometer
    Clock
1   Hot plate or stove
1   Metal soup can, #303
1   Ruler
    Adult supervision

Procedure

1. Fill the beaker half full with ice cubes and then add water to the level of the ice cubes. Insert the thermometer, gently swirl it around a couple of times and record the temperature on the 0 line of the Temp. column of the data table on page 43.

Thermometer Rules!

Procedure

2. If using a thermometer is new to you, here's how they work. There should be a colored liquid, probably alcohol, rising up the middle of the thermometer. As the temperature of the liquid in the bulb at the base of the thermometer increases, the molecules start bouncing around more and spread out to have more room. This pushes the liquid up the tube inside the thermometer. As it cools the opposite action takes place—as the molecules become cooler, they get closer, and the need for room to spread out is gone.

Now that you know what the red line is you should have also noticed two sets of numbers—one on each side of the thin, red line. Fahrenheit you probably recognize as the scale of temperature you hear on weather forecasts here in the United States; we use it more regularly. The other scale is the metric version we call Celsius or centigrade; it is used pretty much everywhere else in the world—so much for being "with it" scientifically speaking.

So, here's how it works: Simply place the fat end of the thermometer in the water. Leave it there for about 30 seconds; then lift it up above the water level and look at the top of the red line. The numbers, written in both temperature scales, will be right there for you to read.

3. Turn the hot plate or stove on with adult supervision and record the temperature for every minute in the spaces provided in the data table on the next page. Continue to heat the ice water mixture until the water has boiled for three minutes or more.

4. Once you have observed the transitions from solid to liquid to gas and recorded the temperature in the table on page 43, graph the data that you collected on the next two pages.

Data & Observations

Time	Temp.	Time	Temp.
0		16	
1		17	
2		18	
3		19	
4		20	
5		21	
6		22	
7		23	
8		24	
9		25	
10		26	
11		27	
12		28	
13		29	
14		30	
15		31	

Thermometer Rules!

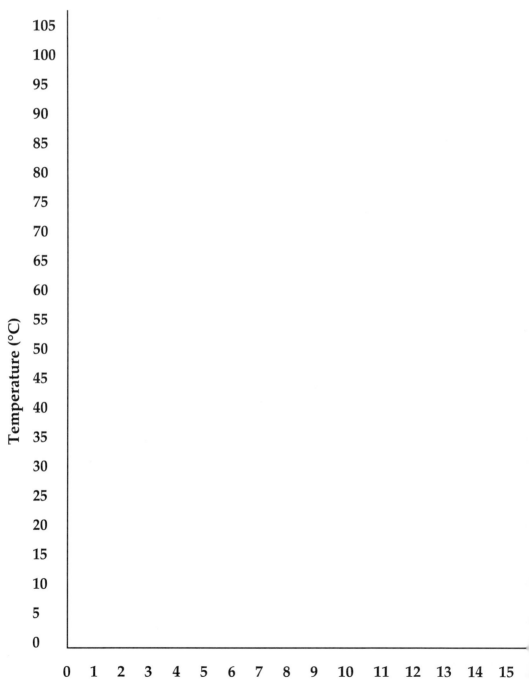

Thermodynamic Thrills • Winholtz, Cramer, Twyman, & Hixson

| 16 | 17 | 18 | 19 | 20 | 21 | 22 | 23 | 24 | 25 | 26 | 27 | 28 | 29 | 30 |

Time (minutes)

Thermometer Rules!

Procedure

5. To continue the process of exploring states of matter take a metal soup can and fill it with ice cubes and then add water until the can is full. Place a thermometer in the can and record the temperature of the water below.

6. Place the can in a warm spot and observe what happens to the outer sides of the can. Record the temperature of the water when you start to see drops of water forming on the outside of the can. This water appears on the outside of the can because water in the air, called water vapor, comes in contact with the cold surface of the can and condenses there. The same process creates clouds in the sky.

Data & Observations

The starting temperature for the can was _____ °C.

The moisture appeared on the can at _____ °C.

How Come, Huh?

When you graphed out the data, you should have noticed that the temperature of the ice water did not change very much as the ice was melting. This is represented by a fairly flat line starting out your graph.

Once all of the ice had melted and changed to liquid water, the temperature started to rise. It continued to rise until the water approached the boiling point.

As the water started to boil, the graphing line once again leveled off meaning that the temperature of the solution remained the same. This is how chemists identify the transition points of different compounds. Once the temperature line levels off, the transition point has been reached.

Science Fair Extensions

14. Experiment with recording and determining the melting point of several soft solids, like butter, lard, or Crisco.

15. Experiment with recording and determining the boiling point of several liquids of your choice. Be sure to have an adult approve your choices—stay away from flammable liquids like gasoline, acetone, mineral spirits, and other liquids that may produce toxic or flammable fumes.

16. Explore the idea of sublimation. Find out what it is and what it has to do with the states of matter and how they transition. With an adult to guide you, explore dry ice and caffeine—two compounds that sublimate very easily.

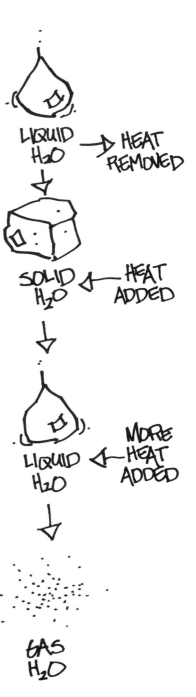

LIQUID H₂O → HEAT REMOVED

SOLID H₂O ← HEAT ADDED

LIQUID H₂O ← MORE HEAT ADDED

GAS H₂O

Liquid Thermometer

The Experiment

A Pyrex test tube full of colored water is plugged with a one-hole stopper that has a tall, glass tube inserted in it. A piece of index card is taped to the glass tube and the entire apparatus is plunged into an ice water bath. When it appears that the colored liquid will not contract any more, the water level in the tube is marked on the index card. The tube is then plunged in a bath of boiling water. Again, when it appears that the water in the tube will not expand anymore, the water level in the tube is marked on the index card.

Using a metric ruler and the two markings that were recorded on the index card, you will be able to create your own homemade thermometer.

Materials

1   #2, One-hole stopper
1   16-inch Piece of 3 mm glass tubing
    Petroleum jelly
1   16 mm x 150 mm Pyrex test tube
1   Bottle of food coloring
1   6-inch by 4-inch Piece of index card
1   Roll of masking tape
3   500-mL beakers
    Hot water
1   Test tube holder
1   Pencil
    Cold water with ice
1   Metric ruler
    Adult supervision

Procedure

1. Slide the glass tubing inside the one-hole stopper. If you have a little petroleum jelly or oil, both those liquids lubricate the glass and make it easier to slide into the stopper.

2. Prepare your "thermometer" by filling the test tube to the top with colored water. Place the stopper on top of the tube and push so it goes approximately halfway into the test tube. The colored water will be pushed up into the tubing. Tape the index card to the tubing so a scale can be marked onto the card as needed. Use the illustration to the right as a guide.

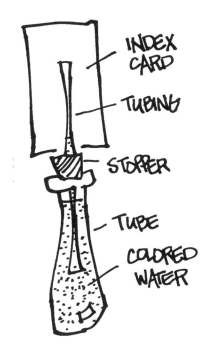

3. Fill one beaker with very hot water—boiling water if it is possible and if you have an adult peeking over your shoulder.

4. Place the test tube in the hot water. Use the illustration to the left as a guide. The water inside the tube will start to expand. When the liquid in the tubing stops moving upward, mark it, and label it 100 degrees C.

Liquid Thermometer

5. Remove the test tube while you prepare an ice bath. Once the bath is ready, plunge the test tube into the cold water. When the water is done moving down the tube, mark it and label it 0 degrees C.

6. Remove the test tube from its ice bath. Measure the distance between the two markings and make 10 evenly spaced marks. The number 100 will represent the hot water mark and 0 for the ice water mark.

7. You now have your own homemade thermometer! Using the metric ruler divide the distance between the two marks by 10. Each mark represents 10 degrees.

How Come, Huh?

As the temperature of the colored liquid rises in the hot bath, the molecules in the tube spread out and have nowhere to go but up the tube—making the water level rise. The opposite is true when it is plunged into its ice bath. The molecules start becoming cozy together; they are cold so they huddle together, the volume of water decreases, and the level drops.

Science Fair Extensions

17. Substitute other liquids, dyed rubbing alcohol, cooking oil, and so on. Be sure to get your parent's permission first.

18. Try using different diameter tubing.

LC Thermometer

The Experiment

The last of the thermometers that we want to introduce you to is relatively new on the scene. It incorporates liquid crystals, reflected light, and the heat produced by your body.

Materials

1 Liquid crystal thermometer
1 Mirror
1 Watch with a sweep-second hand
1 Forehead

Procedure

1. The liquid crystal thermometer, which you are going to use, has been calibrated, or set, to respond to a small temperature range, about 5 degrees above normal and about 5 degrees below normal.

2. While you are sitting, place the liquid crystal thermometer on your forehead with the numbers facing away from your skin. Then take a look at it; note the color and temperature that is recorded on the thermometer and enter that data on the next page.

3. Run around your house, yard, or school for 3 minutes without stopping. If you cannot run around, then do jumping jacks or run in place. The main idea is work up a sweat.

4. Stop exercising and place the thermometer on your forehead again. Note the color and temperature that is recorded on the thermometer and enter that data on the next page.

LC Thermometer

Data & Observations

Enter the color and temperature in the appropriate boxes.

Activity	Color	Temperature
Sitting		
Exercise		

How Come, Huh?

Liquid crystals are fairly complicated and require more space to explain than we have here, but we will try to give you a bit of a head start. Liquid crystals are long, rod-shaped crystals that line up in a single direction. When they are placed between two polarizing filters, the light enters the filter, bends a little, bounces off the liquid crystals, and leaves the surface in a different place.

Temperature affects the liquid crystals, causing them to rotate. As they rotate, the light coming in through the filter is reflected at different wavelengths, producing different colors.

These thermometers are set to respond in a specific temperature range. When you place them on your head, the heat from your body causes the liquid crystals to rotate; and as they rotate, they reflect different colors of light.

Science Fair Extensions

19. Compare the reading of an LC thermometer with a traditional one.

Big Idea 3

When the temperature of a material increases, the motion of the atoms in that material also increases. When the temperature decreases, the speed of the molecules also decreases.

SLG Models

The Experiment

Just saying the words "atomic theory of matter" can make your I.Q. inflate exponentially. Well, maybe not, but knowing that it means atoms are always in motion—smashing and bashing into one another and their surroundings—can help you get your brain pumped and primed. This simple model can show how the atoms in solids, liquids, and gases act and react to temperature change.

Materials

2	Plastic strawberry baskets
4	Twist ties
12	Small Styrofoam balls, 1-inch diameter
1	Multispeed hair dryer

BASKET

BALLS

BASKET

Procedure

1. Place the Styrofoam balls in one of the two berry baskets. Place the other basket over the top to create a cage so the balls will not escape. Use the twist ties to secure the two baskets together.

2. Hold the "molecule cage" above the blower, but do not turn the blower on. Indulge us a bit, this is going to be our model for a solid material.

3.   To demonstrate the action of the molecules trapped in the basket as heat is added, turn the blower on low and observe as the balls begin to randomly bounce throughout the cage. Move the hair dryer back and forth a bit. This is our liquid state.

4.   To represent the gas phase, turn the blower on high and watch the chaotic molecules speed up as the temperature is increased. If you are playing along, this would be our gas phase. We don't do plasma with this model.

Data & Observations

1.   Circle the word that best describes the actions of the Styrofoam balls representing their 3 states of matter.

Solid (before the blower was added):

Still   Slight Movement   Bouncing Around   Chaos

Liquid (the blower set to a low speed):

Still   Slight Movement   Bouncing Around   Chaos

Gas (the blower on a high speed):

Still   Slight Movement   Bouncing Around   Chaos

SLG Models

2. How would you describe the sound and the number of hits on the sides of the cage as the speed of the blower increased?

Got Noisier   *Got Quieter*

3. Did the pressure increase on the walls of the cage or decrease as the speed of the "molecules" got faster?

Increased   *Decreased*

How Come, Huh?

In the first model (representing a solid substance), the balls in the basket did not move very much. If we could see atoms in real life, they would be like that.

Next comes the liquid state. The dryer is turned on low and the balls start to move around freely. They bounce into the sides of the basket more often (this is called pressure) and are more fluid.

Finally, we crank the dryer up to high and the balls are flying everywhere. They slam into the sides of the basket, increasing the pressure inside, and fly all around. This is our gas phase.

Science Fair Extensions

20. Figure out a way to demonstrate this same process using BBs in a petri dish, on an overhead projector.

21. Try making a model on a larger scale using chicken wire and Ping-Pong balls. The one caution that we have when it comes to Ping-Pong balls is that the heat from the dryer can warp the balls. Use a dryer that has a cool setting.

Ink Races

FOOD COLORING

The Experiment

Rumor has it that the temperature of a liquid will directly affect the speed that a dye or drop of food coloring in that liquid will diffuse or spread out.

Since we believe this statement to be largely accurate, we are going to help you set up an experiment to demonstrate this very idea using two Toobes (acrylic cylinders with plastic bottoms available from Loose in the Lab)—one full of hot water and the other cold—and a little food coloring.

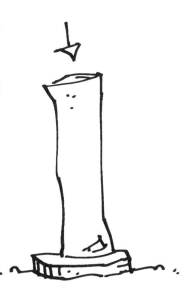

Materials

2   Toobes or other large glasses
1   Bottle of food coloring
    Water, cold
    Water, hot

Ink Races

Procedure

1. Fill one Toobe or other container with very hot water and the other Toobe with very cold water.

2. Place one drop of food coloring in each of the respective Toobes at as nearly the same time as is possible.

3. Observe the movement of the food coloring every minute. Record the perimeters of the ink drops as they expand, using a dotted line, in the spaces provided below.

Data & Observations

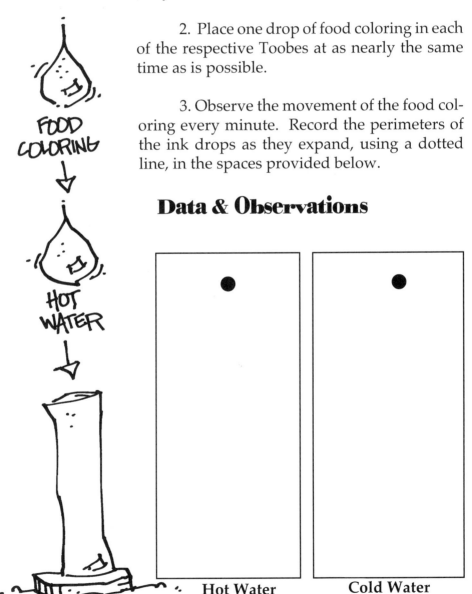

FOOD COLORING

HOT WATER

Hot Water   Cold Water

How Come, Huh?

In the first part of the experiment, the food coloring is heavier than the water, so it diffuses down into it over time. The second part of the experiment has to do with the density of liquids when they are heated. As water molecules are heated, they bump around more, need to spread out, and as a consequence, take up more room. A chemist would say that the liquid became less dense, or the same number of molecules took up more space.

Think of a sack of marbles. When all of the marbles are in the sack, they are crammed very close together. They are very dense. If you empty them out onto the floor, they spread out. Same number of marbles, just taking up more room—less dense.

Warmer liquids that are less dense tend to rise if they are surrounded by colder liquids. This is called a convection current. In this case the warm water in the bottle was less dense than the cold water in the Toobe so it migrated to the top.

Science Fair Extensions

22. Design an experiment to demonstrate that the greater the difference in temperature between the warm water in the bottle and the cold water in the Toobe, the faster the water rises to the top.

23. Change the shape of the warm water container and see if the experiment is altered in any way.

24. Try this same experiment with different liquids.

Dancing Teddies

The Experiment

The tap-dancing dimes is up first and builds on the idea that air is matter and it also produces a force that can be observed when this matter is heated or cooled.

Materials

1   12-oz. Glass pop bottle
1   Freezer or tub of ice water
1   Pie tin with hot water
1   Dime
     Water

Procedure

1. Check the top of your bottle to make sure that it is not chipped. You will need smooth, even surfaces for this experiment to work.

2. Place the bottle in a freezer or tub with ice water for about 10 minutes.

3. Take the pop bottle out of the freezer, or ice water bath, wet the mouth of the bottle, and place a dime squarely on the top. Do not leave any spaces where you can see down into the bottle. Place this bottle in a pie tin that has been filled with hot water. Observe the movement of the dime very carefully.

How Come, Huh?

In this experiment the air inside the bottle was cold. Cold molecules do not have as much energy, so they do not move around as much. If they don't move around as much, they take up less space so more molecules can fit inside the bottle. By cooling the bottle, you are filling it with extra molecules of air.

When you placed the cool bottle—with lots of extra molecules of air in it—into a warm water bath, you started to heat the air inside the bottle. This caused the molecules to start to have more energy, to bounce around a bit more, and to take up more room. There was more air inside the bottle than there was space for all these molecules at room temperature so the pressure inside the bottle started to increase. When it got high enough, the dime was lifted up and some of the air molecules escaped. This continued until there was a balance of forces inside and out of the bottle.

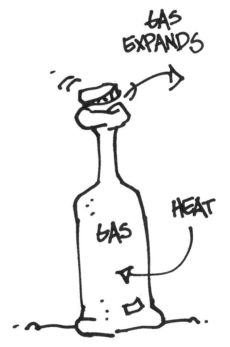

Science Fair Extensions

25. Instead of a dime, place a rubber stopper firmly in the opening of the bottle. Make sure the bottle is very cold when you stopper it and that you place it in hot water.

26. Reverse the process of the lab and see if you can get the dime to stick to the top of the bottle so well that you can't pry it off using your fingers.

Campfire on Command

The Experiment

Two chemicals are going to be added to one another. As they start to react with one another, you will see an exothermic reaction (one that produces heat). The chemicals will start to smoke and then burst into flames. Definitely cool.

Materials

1   Paper towel
1   Tart pan
1   Bottle of glycerin
1   Bottle of potassium permanganate
1   Spoon
    Adult supervision required
    Eye protection recommended
    Well-ventilated area

Procedure

1. Wet the paper towel and place the tart pan upside down on the center of it. This will absorb the heat that is produced and not leave a mark on your counter or table. <u>You should be either outside or in a well-ventilated area.</u>

2. Pour a pile of potassium permanganate about the size of a silver dollar onto the pie tin. Make a small indentation with a spoon, pencil, or other object so the pile of powder now looks like a volcano.

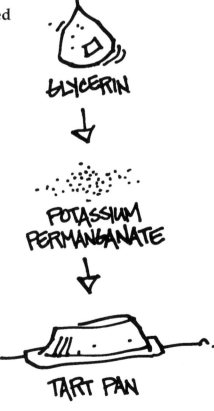

GLYCERIN

POTASSIUM PERMANGANATE

TART PAN

3. Put goggles on, and with an adult present, fill the opening of the volcano with glycerin and stand back. The reaction takes between 20 and 60 seconds to get going. It will smoke first and then burst into flames that will shoot about a foot high. It is best to observe this reaction from the side.

4. When the reaction is complete, wrap everything up in the paper towel, soak it with water, and toss it in the garbage.

How Come, Huh?

As the glycerin (the clear liquid) is absorbed by the potassium permanganate (the purple powder), the atoms in the powder start to react with the atoms in the liquid. As the atoms split apart, they release the energy that held them together. There is enough energy to start a fire.

Science Fair Extensions

27. A general principle of chemistry is that for every 10 degrees Celsius that you increase the temperature of a reaction, the rate of the reaction doubles. In other words, the hotter the chemicals, the faster they react with one another. Design an experiment where you heat and cool the glycerin and test this idea, with adult supervision.

28. Commercial hand and toe warmers are sold during the winter in cold climates. Find out how these work, what chemicals are involved, and how much heat can be produced.

Instant Cold Pack

The Experiment

This experiment allows you to demonstrate one of the characteristics of a chemical reaction—the absorption of heat energy. It is called an endothermic reaction. It is easy to identify this kind of reaction because it is cold to the touch. In this case, ammonium nitrate (famous for being a component of fertilizer) absorbs heat from the room when it is dissolved in water. The temperature of the water can be lowered as much as 16 degrees Fahrenheit, which also makes this a great compound for emergency cold packs.

Materials

1   1-oz. Bottle of ammonium nitrate pellets
1   Baggie
    Water
    Fingers

Procedure

1. Open the bottle of ammonium nitrate and fill the cap with the pellets. Empty the cap full of pellets into the baggie and recap your bottle. Neatness counts.

2. Pinch the ammonium nitrate through the baggie and feel for a temperature change. One would correctly assume at this point that there should be no noticeable difference in temperature.

3. Using room-temperature water, pour a small amount into the baggie—enough to fill it about one-quarter full. Tip the bag back and forth to dissolve the pellets and at the same time feel the sides of the baggie. You should note a significant temperature change.

4. When you are all done, either empty the contents of the bag down the drain or go find a brown spot on the grass and fertilize the yard.

How Come, Huh?

When the water is added to the ammonium nitrate, the ions of the ammonium and nitrate dissolve into the water, and heat is absorbed during the making of the ionic bonds. This type of reaction is known as an endothermic reaction in the science world because heat is absorbed. In this reaction the temperature of the water can be lowered as much as 16° F.

HEAT ABSORBED

Science Fair Extensions

29. Keep the volume of ammonium nitrate the same, record the temperature after the same amount of time, use the same volume of water but change the temperature by 10 degrees each time. See if the reduction in temperature is the same each time.

30. Commercial ice packs are sold in first-aid and home emergency kits. Find out how these work, what chemicals are involved, and how cold they get.

Big Idea 4

Heat is measured in units called calories. The more mass an object has the more heat it can store. The amount of heat an object can absorb is measured as its specific heat.

Calculating Calories

The Experiment

If you are fresh from the previous section, you know that temperature is defined as the average amount of heat in an object and is measured with a thermometer. It makes no difference if the object is large, like the atmosphere, or small, like a spark that shoots out of the fire and onto your bare leg at summer camp.

To measure the amount of heat that is contained in an object, we need to introduce two new terms to you, *calorie* and *specific heat*. The number of calories in an object is the amount of heat an object contains regardless of its mass. Specific heat is the ability of that kind of object to store heat. This series of labs have been adapted from Robert Gardner's book *Science Projects about Temperature and Heat.* Calories first.

Materials

- 3   250-ml Beakers
-     Water
- 1   Burner stand
- 1   Thermometer
- 1   Alcohol burner
- 1   Book of matches
- 1   Clock with sweep-second hand
- **Adult supervision**

Procedure

1. Fill each of the beakers with 100 ml of room-temperature water. Let the beakers stand for a couple of minutes so that the water has a chance to come to a consistent temperature.

Calculating Calories

2. Place the first beaker on the burner stand. Place the thermometer in the water and record the temperature in the data table on the next page.

3. With the supervision of an adult, light the alcohol burner and place it under the beaker. Allow the burner to heat the water for exactly one minute.

4. Remove the burner and place the cap on the wick to extinguish the flame. Swirl the water with the thermometer to mix it well and record the end temperature in the data table.

5. Repeat this experiment with the second beaker of water, heating the water for two minutes and then a third time for three minutes. Record beginning and ending temperatures in the data table as before. When you are done, subtract the end temperature from the initial temperature to get the change in temperature. Enter that data.

6. The big question now is "How much heat was added to each beaker?" To figure this out scientists dug a unit of measure, called a calorie, out of the science measurement closet. To determine the amount of heat that was added you simply multiply the mass of the water (in grams) times the volume of the water (in milliliters).

Helpful hints to move forward:

1 ml of water weighs 1 gram

100 ml of water must weigh _____ grams

Data & Observations

Use the data table below to record the data that you collected in this experiment and determine the change in temperature.

Volume of Water	Heating Time (Minutes)	Beginning Temp.	Ending Temp.	Temp. Change
100 ml	1			
100 ml	2			
100 ml	3			

To calculate the amount of heat, or number of calories added to each beaker of water, use this equation:

Heat (calories) = **Mass of Water** (grams) x **Temp. Change** ($^{\circ}$C)

Using that equation plug your data into the equations outlined below and calculate the amount of heat that was added for each experiment that you performed. Remember, 1 milliliter of water weighs 1 gram.

1. _____ (calories) = ___*100*___ (g) x_____ ($^{\circ}$C)

2. _____ (calories) = _____ (g) x_____ ($^{\circ}$C)

3. _____ (calories) = _____ (g) x_____ ($^{\circ}$C)

Calculating Calories

How Come, Huh?

What you should have determined is that the amount of heat calories added to the second beaker was double the first. The amount of heat energy added to the third beaker should have been triple that of the original beaker.

This lab very clearly demonstrates that the same volume of a material can hold different amounts of heat. Each beaker contained 100 ml of water, but the temperature of the three beakers was quite different. We know this is true because the amount of heat (measured as calories) was different.

Science Fair Extensions

31. With adult supervision, use different sources of heat to provide the calories needed to increase the temperature of the water. Instead of an alcohol burner try a votive candle, a hot plate, a Bunsen burner, an electric stove element, a gas stove burner, and a microwave. Determine the number of calories of heat that each source of heat produces in one minute. Then determine the cost of that heat to see which method is most ecomonical to use.

32. Substitute different kinds of liquids. Try cooking oil, vinegar, sugar water, and so on. Be sure to weigh the liquid to determine the correct weight and calories. Only water can be calculated as one milliliter equaling one gram of weight.

Skinny Pins & Fat Bolts

The Experiment

We know that adding different amounts of heat to the same volume of water will produce different temperatures. This lab is the same idea in reverse. You are going to use the same material, iron, in different quantities to prove that the mass of the object determines the amount of heat it can store.

Materials

1   Straight pin
1   Carriage bolt and nut
1   250-ml Beaker
1   Hot plate
2   100-ml Beakers
2   Thermometers
1   Clock with sweep-second hand
1   Oven mit
1   Pair of tongs
     Water

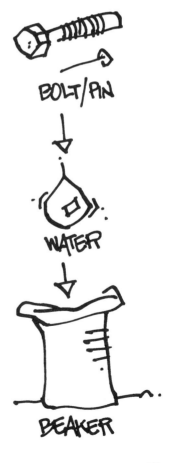

BOLT/PIN

WATER

BEAKER

Procedure

1. Place the straight pin and carriage bolt, both made of iron, in the 250-ml beaker. Add 200 ml of water.

2. Place the 250-ml beaker with the pin and bolt on the hot plate and bring the water to a boil for 3 minutes.

3. While the water is heating, add 100 ml of water to each of the 100-ml beakers. Measure the beginning temperature of each beaker and record that data in the data table on the next page.

Skinny Pins & Fat Bolts

4. At the conclusion of the 3 minutes, empty the hot water into the sink and quickly place the bolt in one beaker and the pin in the other. Let them sit in the beakers for two minutes. At the end of two minutes record the ending temperature for both beakers.

Data & Observations

Use the data table below to record the data that you collected in this experiment, and then determine the amount of heat contained in both the pin and the bolt.

Source of Heat	Heating Time (Minutes)	Beginning Temp.	Ending Temp.	Temp. Change
Pin	2			
Bolt	2			

To calculate the amount of heat, or number of calories added to each beaker of water, use this equation:

Heat (calories) = **Mass of Water** (grams) x **Temp. Change** (ºC)

Using that equation plug your data into the equations outlined below and calculate the amount of heat that was added for each experiment that you performed. Remember, 1 milliliter of water weighs 1 gram.

Pin: _____ (calories) = ___*100*___ (g) x_____ (ºC)

Bolt: _____ (calories) = _____ (g) x_____ (ºC)

How Come, Huh?

This lab gives you hard data to support the argument that the amount of heat that can be stored in an object is directly tied to the mass of the object. The bigger the object, the more heat it can store.

In this case we had two items, a pin and bolt, made out of the same material, iron. They were both heated to the same, exact temperature, 100 ºC, in boiling water and then added to two beakers, each containing 100 ml of water for the same amount of time. The only thing different in the two experiments is the amount of iron—a skinny pin in one beaker and a fat bolt in the other. The bolt, containing more calories of heat, produced a higher temperature in its beaker.

Science Fair Extensions

33. Use different materials—a copper wire and a copper penny, a brass thumbtack and a brass rod, or a nickel and five nickels—to support the idea of mass determining the amount of heat added to a container.

34. Test this theory using liquids. Design an experiment where you are adding different amounts of hot water to a fixed amount of cool water. Record the temperature changes and determine which beaker contained more calories.

35. Prove that a glass of hot water will reach room temperature faster than a bucket of hot water. Why?

Heat Sponges

The Experiment

Before we get to the final idea in this section, specific heat, we need to tuck one more building block into our foundation—heat capacity.

Heat capacity is the ability of a material to absorb and hang onto heat. The more heat (calories) it takes to raise the temperature of an object the greater its heat capacity. For example, water has a heat capacity twice that of cooking oil—and with that factoid the table has been set for the next lab activity.

Materials

2   250-ml Beakers
1   Graduated cylinder
1   Alcohol burner
1   Burner stand
1   Book of matches
1   Clock with sweep-second hand
1   Thermometer
    100 ml Water
    100 ml Cooking oil
    Adult supervision

Procedure

1. Fill one beaker with 100 ml (100g) of water and a second beaker with 112 ml of cooking oil (100g). The graduated cylinder is there to help you with more precise measurement.

2. Place the first beaker with water on the burner stand. Place the thermometer in the water and record the temperature in the data table on page 76.

3. With the supervision of an adult, light the alcohol burner and place it under the beaker. Allow the burner to heat the water for exactly three minutes.

4. Remove the burner and place the cap on the wick to extinguish the flame. Swirl the water with the thermometer to mix it well and record the end temperature in the data table.

5. Repeat this experiment with the second beaker of cooking oil, heating the oil for three minutes also. Record beginning and ending temperatures in the data table as before. When you are done, subtract the end temperature from the initial temperature to get the change in temperature. Enter that data.

6. The big question now is "How much heat was absorbed by each liquid?" This is called the heat capacity of the liquid. To figure this out, scientists, we have another formula for you to use:

Heat Capacity (cal/$^{\circ}$C)= **Heat Absorbed** (cal)/**Temp. Change** ($^{\circ}$C)

Data & Observations

To determine the heat capacity of the liquid you need to first calculate the amount of heat absorbed. This is straight out of the last two labs and should be a cakewalk for you now.

Heat Sponges

Type of Liquid	Heating Time (Minutes)	Beginning Temp.	Ending Temp.	Temp. Change
Water	3			
Oil	3			

To calculate the amount of heat, or number of calories added to each beaker, use this equation:

Heat (calories) = **Mass of Liquid** (grams) x **Temp. Change** (ºC)

Using that equation for reference, plug your data into the equations outlined below and calculate the amount of heat that was added for each experiment that you performed.

1. _____ (calories) = ___*100*___ (g) x_____ (ºC)

2. _____ (calories) = _____ (g) x_____ (ºC)

You're almost there—you now know the number of calories and you can find the temperature change in the data table above. Plug in the numbers and multiply to find the heat capacity.

Heat Capacity (calories/ºC)= **Heat Absorbed** (cal)/**Temp. Change** (ºC)

1. _____ Water = _____ (cal)/ _____ (ºC)

2. _____ Oil = _____ (cal)/ _____ (ºC)

How Come, Huh?

You saw from your data that the *temperature*, the average amount of heat, of the oil was almost twice the temperature of the water. What this means is that it takes twice as much heat to raise the temperature of the water as it does to raise the temperature of the oil to the same reading. Water has a higher capacity to absorb heat: It takes more. Another way of looking at this is that if the same amount of heat were added to the same mass of two different liquids, the ability to absorb the heat would not be the same and therefore the final temperature would not be the same.

With that last tidbit of physics trivia in our footlocker we can now finally bring this chapter to a close with a lab specifically on specific heat—to be exact.

Science Fair Extensions

36. Interchange several kinds of liquids and determine the heat capacity of each one using the method outlined in this lab. Place them in order from best heat sponge to worst.

37. Not only do oil and water have different heat capacities, but they are also different densities. Place an ice cube in a beaker of oil and observe and explain what happens as the ice cube melts and changes to water.

38. Leading into the next lab, which will melt an ice cube faster, a cup of cold water or an empty cup?

Heat, to be Specific

The Experiment

This is the culminating activity in this section, so, if you have been skipping around, this is a good time to retreat to page 67 and build your foundation.

Specific heat is defined as the amount of heat (in calories) that it takes to raise 1 gram of matter 1 degree Celsius. The more heat that has to be added to an object to raise its temperature, the higher the specific heat is said to be. If an object heats up quickly, like metal, it has a low specific heat.

SHOT

WAX CUP TO FREEZER

Materials

3   250-ml Beakers
    Water
3   Thermometers
3   5-oz. Wax cups
    100 g Lead BBs
    100 g Copper BBs
    100 g Aluminum BBs
1   Balance
1   Freezer
1   Clock with sweep-second hand

Procedure

1. Fill each of the beakers with 100 ml of room-temperature water. Let the beakers stand for a couple of minutes so that the water has a chance to come to a consistent temperature. Record this temperature in the data table on the next page.

2. Weigh 100 g of iron BBs into a wax cup. Repeat this with the two other cups with 100 g of aluminum and copper shot respectively. Place all three cups in the freezer for 15 minutes.

3. Take all three of the wax cups out of the freezer at the same time and empty one cup into one beaker.

4. Repeat this with the other two wax cups so that you now have three beakers, one with iron, one with aluminum, and one with copper shot in them. Place a thermometer in each beaker and let them stand for 3 minutes.

5. At the end of three minutes record the temperature in each of the three beakers. Do this as quickly as possible.

Data & Observations

Use the data table below to record the data that you collected in this experiment and determine the change in temperature.

Materials	Mass of Metal	Beginning Temp.	Ending Temp.	Temp. Change
Lead	100 g			
Copper	100 g			
Aluminum	100 g			

Heat, to be Specific

To calculate the specific heat, use this equation:

Specific Heat(cal/ºC/g) = **Heat Capacity** (cal/ºC)/**Mass** (g), but

1. First we need to calculate the amount of heat, or number of calories taken from each beaker, use this equation:

Heat (calories) = **Mass** (grams) x **Temp. Change** (ºC)

Using that equation plug your data into the equations outlined below and calculate the amount of heat that was lost for each experiment that you performed.

Lead _____ (calories) = _____ (g) x_____ (ºC)

Copper _____ (calories) = _____ (g) x_____ (ºC)

Aluminum _____ (calories) = _____ (g) x_____ (ºC)

2. Next we need to find the heat capacity.

Heat Capacity (cal/ºC)= **Heat Absorbed**(cal)/**Temp. Change** (ºC)

_____ Lead = _____ (cal)/ _____ (ºC)

_____ Copper = _____ (cal)/ _____ (ºC)

_____ Aluminum= _____ (cal)/ _____ (ºC)

3. And finally, to determine the specific heat, use this equation:

Specific Heat(cal/°C/g) = **Heat Capacity** (cal/°C)/**Mass** (g)

_____ Lead = _____ (cal)/ _____ (g)

_____ Copper = _____ (cal)/ _____ (g)

_____ Aluminum= _____(cal)/ _____ (g)

How Come, Huh?

The interesting thing is that when you did your calculations you should have found that the order and approximate values for specific heat were:

1. Water   1.0
2. Aluminum   0.22
3. Copper   0.092
4. Lead   0.031

If you were to arrange these substances in order of density, this list would be identical. The implication being that the more tightly packed together a material is, the less heat it takes to warm it up. The reason for this is that the atoms are more tightly squished in the more dense materials, and it does not take many bumps to get them going.

Science Fair Extensions

39. When an ice cube melts, the temperature does not change even though you are adding calories. Where does the heat go?

Big Idea 5

Heat always moves from hot to cold. The greater the difference in temperature between two objects, the faster their temperatures change.

Hot-to-Cold Hanger

The Experiment

Heat can move from one place to another three different ways: by conduction, by convection, and by radiation. This lab is going to explore heat conduction in solids. Conduction takes place in solids, liquids, and gases, but it works the best in solids. If we give you the rest of the background information, then there is no sense in having you do the lab because you will already know the answer.

The other point to be made is that a **temperature gradient** will exist from the area of highest temperature to the area of lowest temperature. What this means is that between the high and low temperature extremes, the temperature gets steadily higher from one end to the other. In this experiment, for example, the wire will be hottest at the end in the flame, and the coolest at the end being held. In between it will get progressively cooler from the hot end to the cool end. If the temperature were actually measured at each of the tacks, we would see this as steadily decreasing temperature readings between the two points.

Materials

1   Wire, copper (14 inches) (12-14 gauge)
1   Ruler
1   Marker, felt tip
1   Book of matches
1   Candle
7   Thumbtacks, metal
1   Clock, sweep-second hand
Adult supervision

Hot-to-Cold Hanger

Procedure

1. If it has not already been done, bend the copper wire so that it is as straight as possible and then make an 180-degree bend about four inches from the end to make a small handle. The illustration to the right should help some.

2. Lay the ruler out next to the wire. Use a felt tip marker and make seven marks on the wire at one-inch intervals starting from the end away from the handle, with the first mark two inches from the end.

3. With adult supervision, light the candle and let some of the wax melt. When it has melted, blow the candle out and dip the top of the tack into the wax. Immediately place the wax end of the tack on the wire at the first mark, two inches from the end, and release it. The wax cools quickly so you don't really have to hold it there until it becomes hard.

4. Continue this procedure until you have all seven of the tacks stuck on the wire at each successive mark. Use the illustration on the opposite page to help you out.

5. Light the candle again.

6. Begin heating the wire by holding onto its handle and holding the other end in the flame. As soon as you place the wire in the flame, start a stopwatch or note the time. Note the time when each tack falls off the wire and record it in the data table shown on page 85.

Data & Observations

Record the beginning time at all seven tacks, and then as each tack falls note that time also. Determine the total amount of time it took for each tack to fall—something we call hang time.

Tack #	Beg. Time	End Time	Hang Time
1			
2			
3			
4			
5			
6			
7			

Hot-to-Cold Hanger

How Come, Huh?

Basically what is happening in this lab is you are heating the end of a metal rod that is cold to start with like the rest of the rod, but it becomes hot very quickly. The molecules of metal in the rod start to move faster where the heat is applied. Those molecules bump into the cooler molecules that are next to them in the rod and transfer some of the energy to them, making them move faster. They, in turn, bump into the molecules that are next to them. It's a lot like dominos. You add heat to the first set of molecules, and they pass it on down the line.

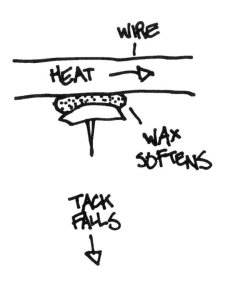

As the heat is applied to the rod, the whole rod gets warmer, the wax softens, and the tacks fall off one at a time. The order of the tacks falling illustrates the movement of the heat down the rod from the hot end of the rod to the cold end—one piece of evidence to support our statement at the beginning of the section.

Science Fair Extensions

40. Apply different kinds of heat to the end of the copper wire. With adult supervision, try placing it on an electric stove, torching it with propane, or clipping a lantern battery to one end. See if the results are the same and compare the speed that the tacks fall from the wire.

41. Substitute different kinds of metal—aluminum, brass, steel, nichrome—and determine if all metals conduct heat from the hot ends to the cold ends.

Thermal Moderation

The Experiment

Two cans containing different temperatures of water can be used to compare the rate of cooling and heating. This addresses the second half of our statement in Big Idea 5: The larger the difference in temperatures between two bodies the quicker the temperature changes.

By placing one can inside of another larger can, the temperature in one can can have quite an effect on the other can. Best of all, the results can be graphed and can be used for further discussion. We promise no more corny can-can jokes.

Materials

1   Plastic tub, 1 gallon
    Water, hot & cool
2   Thermometers
1   10-oz. Soup can, clean
1   48-oz. Metal can, clean
    Ice cubes
1   96-oz. Metal can, clean
1   Clock with sweep-second hand

Procedure

1. Fill the plastic one-gallon tub with 40 ounces of lukewarm water. Insert a thermometer and read the temperature. Add hot water until it comes up to 30 degrees C.

2. Using the 10-oz. soup can fill the smaller (48 oz.) of the two metal cans with 30-degree water. Total volume of water should be 40 ounces or 4 cans. Insert the thermometer in the can and leave it there.

Thermal Moderation

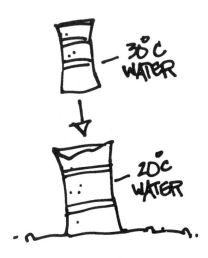

3. Refill the plastic one-gallon tub with 40 ounces of cool water. Insert a thermometer and read the temperature. Add cold water until it comes down to 20 degrees C.

4. Using the 10-oz. soup can fill the larger of the two metal cans (96 oz.) with the 20-degree water. Total volume of water should be 40 ounces or 4 cans. Insert the thermometer in the can and leave it there.

5. Place the smaller, warm water can inside the larger, cold water can. Record the temperature of the smaller can every minute in the data table for 10 minutes or until there is no longer a change. Between readings, use the thermometers in the cans to stir the water around to make sure that the heat is being evenly distributed.

6. Repeat this experiment increasing the temperature difference between the two cans each time. You started with 20º C and 30º C. On the second go around use 10º C and 40º C, and on the final go around use 0º C and 50º C. Record all data in the data tables provided.

7. After you have recorded the temperature changes in the small can under all three conditions, plot the data as a graph on page 90. Use the graph to answer the questions that follow.

Data & Observations

Temperature Table

Time (minutes)	Lab #1	Lab #2	Lab #3
1	30º C	40º C	50º C
2			
3			
4			
5			
6			
7			
8			
9			
10			

1. When did the fastest temperature changes take place?
   Toward the: beginning   middle   end

2. When did the temperature change the least?
   Toward the: beginning   middle   end

3. Graph the temperatures you recorded in the data table above.

Thermal Moderation

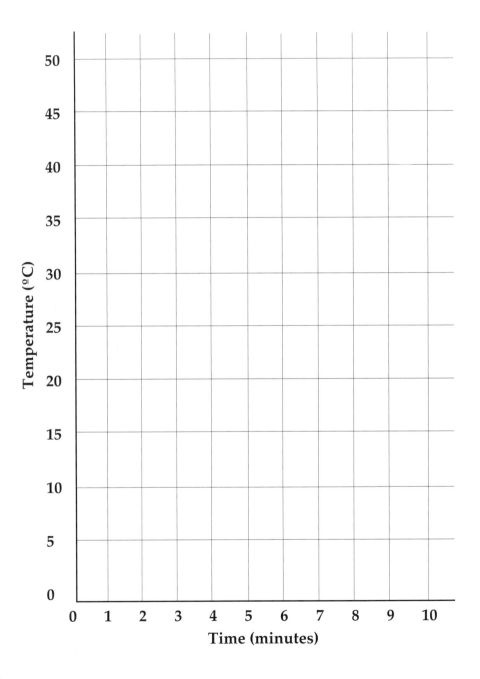

How Come, Huh?

The Rules of Temperature Change:

1. When objects of different temperatures are in contact with one another, the warmer one gets cooler and the cooler one gets warmer. They share the heat.

2. The bigger the difference in temperature between the two objects, the quicker the temperature changes. The more heat there is to share, the faster it is shared. You should have noticed that the hotter the water was when it started, the steeper the curve was showing it cooling off.

3. Finally, the bigger the object, the more mass it has, and the more influence it will have on the other object's temperature—and the less its own temperature will change. Really big, hot things will share their heat with little cold things and not lose much heat in the process and vice versa for really big, cold things and little tiny, hot things. We did not prove that one, but you can now develop an extension that will take you where you need to go.

Science Fair Extensions

42. Rather than using equal amounts of water, change the volumes to favor either the cold or the hot. This ties to rule of temperature number 3 above.

43. Reverse the temperatures in the containers; then try it again and see if you get the same results. Does it make a difference if the cold is on the outside or the inside?

44. Change the experiment so that you are actually mixing the two batches of water rather than having the heat conduct through the wall of a can.

Expandable Balloons

The Experiment

We know that heat will travel down from the hot end of the wire to the cool end and that water will pass heat from hot to cold. What about air? This experiment is going to answer that question using a clean pop bottle, a balloon, and a bath of hot water.

Materials

1   Balloon
1   Clean, 32-oz. pop bottle
1   Plastic tub, 3 gallon
     Hot water
     Ice cubes

Procedure

1.   Place the balloon over the neck of the bottle. It should be limp and have as little air in it as possible.

2.   Fill the plastic tub with very hot water, as hot as you can get from the faucet. The tub should be about two-thirds full.

3.   Place the pop bottle in the plastic tub in an upright position. Use the illustration to the right as a guide. The water in the water bath will heat the air inside the bottle. Draw a picture of your balloon, over the bottle on the next page.

4.   Empty the water down the drain and refill the tub with cold water, add ice cubes. Place the pop bottle with the inflated balloon in the ice water. Note the reaction.

Data & Observations

Draw a picture of the pop bottle once it has been in the hot water for 5 minutes or so.

How Come, Huh?

The heat in the hot water was conducted through the plastic and into the air inside the bottle. This heated the air inside causing it to expand. As the air expanded, it was looking for more space so it expanded into the balloon and inflated it.

When you placed the pop bottle in ice water, the air inside the bottle started to contract. As it did, it needed less room so the balloon deflated and went limp to the point of possibly being pushed inside the pop bottle as the air cooled to near freezing temperature.

Science Fair Extensions

45. Put the pop bottle in the freezer for about 10 minutes. Take the bottle out and place a balloon over the opening. Set the bottle in a warm room and observe the balloon.

Big Idea 6

Insulation is the ability of a material to prevent the movement of heat.

Insulation Pockets

The Experiment

Heat is always on the lookout for an adventure to a cooler spot, kind of like a person who lives in Arizona in July. Sometimes this is a good thing, but more often than not it is not such a good thing. When we pay to heat our houses, we want to be as energy efficient as possible; when we go skiing in the winter, we would like to stay warm. There are lots of occasions where we would prefer to prevent heat loss or gain using insulation.

This lab allows you to explore the ability of different kinds of materials to prevent the movement of heat.

Materials

1   Sheet of bubble wrap
1   Old newspaper
1   Flannel blanket
1   Sheet of aluminum foil
1   Cardboard box
1   Pair of scissors
1   Ruler
1   Roll of masking tape
5   Thermometers
1   Clock with second hand

Procedure

1. Prepare 5 pockets using the materials listed in the section above. Each pocket should be made from a sheet that is 12 inches wide and 9 inches tall. Fold the pockets in half to a finished size of 6 inches wide and 9 inches tall.

2. Tape the pockets along the side and bottom to seal them off, but be sure to leave the top open for the thermometer.

Insulation Pockets

3. Insert the thermometers in the openings of all five of the pockets. Take a temperature reading after one minute and record that information in the data table below.

4. Take all five of the pockets out into the sun. Record the temperature and start the clock running. Record the temperature of each pocket, every minute for 10 minutes.

5. Gather all the pockets up and go quickly inside. Place the pockets on a table away from the sun. Record the temperature of the pockets as they cool down and record that data in the table on the opposite page.

Data & Observations

Heating Insulation Pockets

Time	0	1	2	3	4	5	6	7	8	9	10
B. Wrap											
Alum.											
C-board											
Flannel											
News											

Cooling Insulation Pockets

Time	0	1	2	3	4	5	6	7	8	9	10
B. Wrap											
Alum.											
C-board											
Flannel											
News											

How Come, Huh?

The materials that insulated the most effectively had the lowest temperature increase. Those items that were poor insulators had a rapid increase.

When you brought the same items inside, the poor insulators cooled quickly while the good insulators took their time.

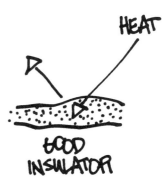

GOOD INSULATOR

Science Fair Extensions

46. Use other materials that are advertised by outdoor clothing companies to be good insulators. Devise a test that will allow you to do some consumer testing for truth in selling.

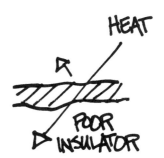

POOR INSULATOR

Soup-Can Races

The Experiment

Design a blanket and lid for a soup can that will keep hot water in the can hot. To make it exciting, have a race with a friend to see whose insulator slows the heat loss for the longest amount of time. You want to be s-l-o-w in this race. The tortoise rules!

Materials

    Insulating material
1   Hot plate
1   2-qt. Saucepan
1   Graduated cylinder, 250 ml
1   Thermometer per team
1   Clock
1   #303 Soup can per team
    200 ml of hot water per team
2   Hot pads
1   Friend
    Adult supervision

Procedure

1. Design a blanket and lid for the can from available materials. Remember, you will need to be able to read a thermometer stuck through the lid so be sure to plan for that necessity.

2. Using extreme caution, pour 200 ml of hot water from the saucepan into the graduated cylinder.

3. Immediately pour the 200 ml of water into the soup can and then seal your can up quickly. While you are doing this, have your friend also get 200 ml of water and start recording. Record the beginning temperature and then the temperature every minute for 10 minutes.

Data & Observations

Soup-Can Races

Time	0	1	2	3	4	5	6	7	8	9	10
Temp. Can #1											
Temp. Can #2											

How Come, Huh?

The person who created the most leak-proof, in terms of heat, can, wins! Why? Because they were the best in the field of entrants, that's why.

Science Fair Extensions

47. Have a contest to build the thinnest insulating "blanket and lid."

48. Have a contest to build the insulator with the least amount of mass.

49. Graph the heat loss data collected above over a period of time. Extrapolate the temperature at twelve, fifteen, and twenty minutes.

Big Idea 7

Heat waves can radiate through a vacuum or gas in all directions. Gases expand when they are heated and contract when they are cooled.

Solar Pockets

The Experiment

This experiment is a great excuse to spend the day outside, catch some sunbeams in various colors of paper pockets, and record the temperature changes.

The Sun produces all kinds of electromagnetic waves that are grouped as radiant energy, including visible light and infrared (heat) waves. Different colors react differently to this radiant energy: Some reflect it, others absorb it, and still others do a combination of things. This lab will examine how radiant energy and colors interact with one another.

Materials

5 Thermometers
5 Sheets of paper
     White
     Red
     Blue
     Green
     Black
1 Stapler
1 Clock

Procedure

HOT DOG FOLD

1. Prepare 5 pockets using the colors listed in the Materials section above. Fold a piece of construction paper hot dog length (long and narrow for you nonelementary teacher types). Staple the bottom and side of each pocket.

2. Put the thermometers into the pockets and take them out into the sun. Record the temperature and start the clock running. Record the temperature of each pocket, every minute for 10 minutes.

Solar Pockets

Data & Observations

Heating Colored Pockets

Time	0	1	2	3	4	5	6	7	8	9	10
White											
Red											
Green											
Blue											
Black											

How Come, Huh?

White surfaces reflect white light and as such do not increase in temperature very much. Black surfaces absorb radiant light as well as the infrared light that accompanies it on its journey from the sun. The other colors fit in between the black and white.

Science Fair Extensions

50. Rather than using colored pockets, head to the wrapping store and purchase metallic-coated papers of different hues. Try silver, copper, and gold. Any difference?

Kinetic Balloons

The Experiment

A drop of water is added to a Pyrex test tube and then a rubber balloon is inserted over the mouth of the same tube. The base of this tube is then heated by the flame of a candle. As the contents of the tube are heated, the air molecules begin to bounce around and take up more space—an interesting thing happens to the balloon. However, we are far from finished. The entire apparatus is then plunged in an ice bath, the balloon not only reacts to the temperature change but also in some instances may actually overreact.

Materials

1   16-mm x 150-mm Pyrex test tube
1   Rubber balloon
1   Test tube holder
1   Book of matches
1   Votive candle
1   250-ml Beaker
    Ice
    Water
    Adult supervision

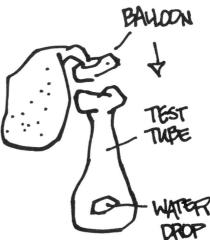

Procedure

1. Place a drop of water into the test tube. It is important that the tube be Pyrex brand. It will be heated and then cooled rapidly. Some kinds of glass will shatter when exposed to these conditions.

2. Fit the rubber balloon over the mouth of the test tube so that it completely encloses the tube. No air can get in or out. Place the tube in the test tube holder. The holder should be positioned in the middle of the clamp.

Kinetic Balloons

3. Under adult supervision light the candle. Position the bottom of the tube over the top of the flame and heat the bottom of the tube. Observe what happens to the balloon. Any evidence that gases expand when they are heated?

4. Once the balloon has inflated, place the bottom half of the test tube in the ice bath. Again, observe what happens to the balloon. From your observations what can you infer, or figure out, happens to gases when they are cooled?

Data & Observations

Circle the answer that best describes what happened.

1. What happens to the air inside the balloon as the air in the test tube is heated?

Gets Hotter   *Stays the Same*   *Gets Cooler*

2. When the air gets hot what happens to the distance between the molecules?

Expands   *Nothing*   *Contracts*

3. When the air gets cold, in the ice bath, what happens to the balloon?

Expands   *Nothing*   *Contracts*

How Come, Huh?

When the air inside the test tube was heated, the molecules of air got very excited by the temperature increase and started moving about more quickly in all directions. Because the balloon trapped the air in the test tube and made it a closed system, the only recourse for the air molecules was to push against the most flexible thing, the balloon, and cause it to expand—our first bit of evidence that air expands when it is heated.

The ice bath had the opposite effect on the molecules of air inside the tube. Once the temperature began to decrease in the tube, the air molecules began to bounce less—they had less energy. The upshot of all this is that they needed less room so they retreated to the bottom of the tube, the balloon shrank, and we have a second piece of evidence about air and how it behaves when it is heated.

Science Fair Extensions

51. Reverse the process. Inflate a balloon and pinch the neck about an inch below the mouth. Fit the mouth of the balloon over the mouth of the test tube. Place it in the freezer for 10-15 minutes and then pull it out and observe what happens.

52. Carbon dioxide is a gas at room temperature, but you can also find it as a solid called dry ice. With adult supervision and tongs, take a piece of dry ice and plunk it in a test tube. Place a balloon over the tube and observe what happens to the balloon. Find out why.

Solar Balloon

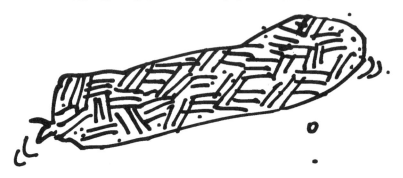

The Experiment

There are several solar hot air balloons available commercially. We enjoy using a balloon manufactured by Delta Education. You can catch up with them at www. delta-education.com or call toll free at 1-800-258-1302.

The balloon inflates to about 12 feet. This is the part where you use your lungs. The balloon is then tied off and placed in the direct sunlight. The black, solar balloon collects and absorbs the sunlight, further heating the air inside, causing it to expand. When the balloon reaches a density that is lighter than the surrounding air, it starts to float.

Materials

1 Solar, hot air balloon
1 Sunny day
1 20-foot string
   Air

Procedure

1. Stretch the balloon out in front of you and start to inflate the balloon by blowing into it.

2. When the balloon is completely inflated, tie it off and take it to a nice, sunny location. The black plastic will immediately begin to absorb the heat energy from the sun, and the air inside the balloon will start to expand—reinforcing two of the ideas that we have already covered in the book.

3. You will notice the balloon starting to float. When the air inside the balloon becomes less dense than the surrounding air outside the balloon, it will float up into the air and be tethered only by the string.

How Come, Huh?

When the difference in density between the air inside the solar balloon and the air outside the balloon gets large enough, the balloon starts to float. The reason for this is that the air molecules expand when they are heated. The expanded air is pushed up by the heavier, denser air outside the balloon.

Science Fair Extensions

53. There are several patterns for tissue paper hot air balloons. These balloons are usually inflated using a hair dryer and kept aloft by burning a small amount of alcohol and constantly filling the balloon with hot air. Be sure to get the permission of an adult to do this.

54. Substitute a dark plastic garbage bag for the solar hot air balloon and see if you can figure a way to get that in the air.

Can Crusher

The Experiment

You can tell your friends that you can crush metal cans simply by looking at them. That's right, crushing them without ever touching them—just apply your patented withering stink eye, and the air pressure in the room. This is done by taking a one-gallon metal can and heating it on a hot plate until the water boils from the opening. The hot can is then quickly capped and placed upright in a tub of ice water. The can is crushed, literally, by the air pressure in our atmosphere.

Materials

1   Plastic container, 2 gallon
1   Cup
1   Cup of ice water
    Water
1   Hot plate
1   Metal, 1 gallon can with screw cap
1   Oven mitt
1   Pair of goggles
    Adult supervision

Procedure

1. Fill the plastic container about one-quarter full of water and toss in a couple of ice cubes for good measure. This is your ice bath.

2. Place a clean, empty, one-gallon metal can on the cold hot plate. Add about a half a cup of water. Let the can sit there for about 30 seconds and observe what happens, if anything.

3. After 30 seconds of sheer boredom, turn the hot plate to high—with adult supervision, of course. The plate will warm up, heating the bottom of the can, causing the water inside the can to boil. When vapor starts coming out of the opening to the can, you are in business.

4. Put on the goggles and the oven mitt and remove the can from the hot plate. Quickly screw the cap onto the can and place it upright in the ice bath. If you want to give the can a stink eye you can, but the air pressure in the room will crush the can for you.

GAS EXPANDS

GAS GETS HOT

HEAT ADDED TO CAN

How Come, Huh?

By heating the can, the water and air molecules inside the can started getting very excited and were bouncing around and off of each other. The heat caused them to move faster, they had more kinetic energy. All this bouncing around caused the air inside the can to expand, and most of these air molecules were shoved out through the top opening of the can. That was the water vapor that you saw. This mass exit sets the stage for the next portion of the experiment.

Can Crusher

When the can was capped, you created a closed system. No air could get in or out of the can. The air pressure outside the can pushing on the water was the same as before, but as the can cooled, the few remaining air molecules contracted, taking up less space. This shrinking of the air molecules created very low pressure inside the can.

This low pressure did not provide much resistance so the air outside pushed on and collapsed the can—much noisier than crushing the can against your forehead and more impressive too.

Science Fair Extensions

55. This experiment also works very well with 16-oz. aluminum cans. Place a small amount of water inside the can, place the can on a stove with adult supervision. Heat the water until it is boiling then remove the can and set it upside down inside an ice bath. You will be very pleased with the results.

56. With adult supervision, light a piece of paper on fire and toss it in a one-gallon pickle jar. Quickly place a water balloon over the mouth of the pickle jar. Make sure the balloon is just a little too big to be pushed into the jar. As the paper burns, the balloon will first dance and then the balloon will be pushed into the jar for the same reasons that the can was crushed.

57. Place a very hot Pyrex test tube upside down in an ice bath. Observe what happens to the water in the ice bath.

Big Idea 8

Heat can travel through gases and liquids as a convection current. Liquids and gases expand when they are heated and contract when they are cooled.

Poor Man's Lava Lamp

The Experiment

To begin exploring the idea of convection currents, we will engage a tricky maneuver of inverting a 2-liter bottle over another one to demonstrate how temperature effects the expansion and contraction of molecules. Have the mop and bucket handy if you are a newcomer to this slight of hand.

Materials

2   2-liter Bottles, clear
    Cold water
    Hot water
1   Bottle of food coloring
1   Tornado Tube
1   Pencil
    Paper

Procedure

1. Fill one of the bottles with cold water to the very top of the opening (the colder the better). Set it aside for now.

2. Fill the other bottle with hot water, as hot as you can stand holding onto. Add a several drops of food coloring to the hot water and be sure it mixes thoroughly. You are looking to produce a dark color.

3. Screw the Tornado Tube (a bottle connector, available at most science and toy stores and in the catalogs listed in this book) onto the top of the bottle with the cold water. When it is firmly in place, quickly flip the whole contraption over and screw it into the bottle with the hot water.

4. Balance the two bottles on the table in front of you and observe what happens to the hot, colored water in the bottom bottle.

Data & Observations

On a separate sheet of paper draw a series of pictures showing the development of the convection current over time. Try drawing a picture every minute for about 5 minutes on a separate piece of paper.

How Come, Huh?

Heat makes things exciting, literally. The molecules of water in the colored, hot water were going crazy trying to spread out from one another. They were trying to become less dense, but had nowhere to go. Once the second pop bottle was screwed on top and a way out was created, they rushed upward. With the cold water above, the cold molecules—being more dense, or heavier—began to fall into the lower bottle helping to put into action the convection current that became visible. The cold water pressing down helped to displace the warm water below—pushing it up. Warm stuff rises and cold stuff falls, that's nature.

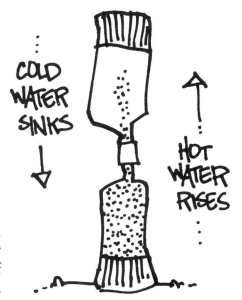

COLD WATER SINKS

HOT WATER RISES

Science Fair Extensions

58. Try varying the temperatures. As you do this, try timing the rate of displacement for the convection current. Do large temperature differences produce larger and quicker convection currents?

59. Try to demonstrate how gas expands and contracts with a helium balloon. Place the balloon in an icebox and compare the before and after. Notice the quick expansion of the helium molecules after you take the balloon out of the icebox and place your nice warm hands around it.

Convection Window

The Experiment

This is a great demonstration to actually show the movement of the cold and warm currents in water. Warm water will rise when heated in the aquarium, which in turn will bend light. There right before your eyes, waving about on the big screen, you will be able to see convection in motion through your convection window

Materials

1   Small aquarium
    Water
1   6 inches of Nichrome wire
1   Pencil
2   Alligator clips
1   Flashlight
1   6-Volt battery
1   Bottle of food coloring
1   White, wall surface

Procedure

1. Fill the aquarium full of water. For this experiment it is better that the water be cool to cold so that the convection currents are more dramatic.

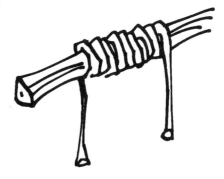

2. Take the nichrome wire and wrap it around the pencil, leaving a one-inch tail on each end. Use the illustration to the right as a guide.

3. Put an alligator clip onto both ends of the nichrome wire. Lower the nichrome loop (horizontally) into the center of the tank full of water. Connect the other end of the leads to the battery.

FLASHLIGHT

4. Place the flashlight in front of the screen and prop it up so that it shines just above the nichrome loop in the tank and onto the back wall.

5. As the electricity starts to flow through the wire, it will become hot. The hot wire will immediately pass the heat, through conduction, to the water molecules that will begin to get warm. The warm water will be pushed up by the heavier, colder water and start to rise in a convection current. Since the water is less dense, the light passing through the warm water will be bent to a different angle than the light passing through the cold water. This produces the effect of waves and shadows that you can see on the wall behind the aquarium.

6. Add a few drops of food coloring to the water and the convection current becomes even more visible. Draw what you see in the box on the next page.

Convection Window

Data & Observations

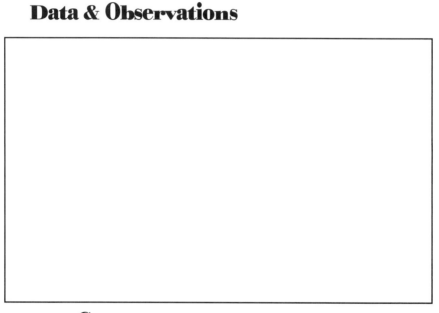

How Come, Huh?

Hot air rises! You know that because you have probably sat at the top of the bleachers in the balcony during a basketball game before and started to sweat. The people closer to the floor seem quite comfortable. The same happens with water. Water will expand as it gets warmer and it will become less dense. The warm water will rise up above the cooler water, and this will set up a convection current. The screen allows you to see the bending of the light waves as they pass through the warm water. Adding food coloring to the aquarium allows you to actually see the warm water rising to the top.

Science Fair Extensions

60. Experiment and see if the voltage of the battery affects the speed that the convection current rises to the top of the aquarium.

61. Try other conductors in place of the nichrome wire loop; for example, nails, wire, copper, and a lightbulb come to mind. Think outside the current.

Convection Tube

The Experiment

There are several ways to approach this idea of a convection current using hot air and cold air and determining which sinks while the other rises. In this particular experiment we are going to recommend a commercially produced glass tube that we have available in our catalog and on our Web site. The tube looks like a giant, fat "O" and has an opening at the top where you add water and a drop of food coloring.

Once the tube is filled you light a votive candle—adult supervision, as always, recommended, and you heat one side of the "O". As the water is heated, it starts to flow in a convection current.

Materials

1   Convection tube
1   Bottle of food coloring
1   Votive candle
     Water
     Adult supervision

Procedure

1. Fill the convection tube with room-temperature water. Add two or three drops of food coloring to one side of the convection tube and try not to disturb the food coloring.

Convection Tube

2. With the supervision of an adult, light a votive candle and hold the side of the tube that has the food coloring directly over the candle flame. Use the illustration as a guide.

How Come, Huh?

As the water was heated, it absorbed the energy from the burning candle. This caused the molecules of water to move back and forth and bounce around more than the molecules of water that were not being heated by the candle. All this bouncing around caused the same number of molecules to expand and take up more space. This made the water less dense. The less dense water was lighter than the cold water and started to rise. As the warm water rose, it left a void and that void was filled by cold water. The cold water got warmer, the warm water got cooler, and this created a convection current.

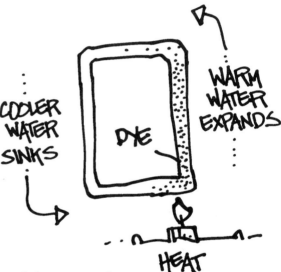

Science Fair Extensions

62. Find other containers that can be heated on one side and set up a convection current. Try a one-gallon jar, an aquarium, and experiment with lots of different shapes and sizes. You may be both pleased and surprised by what you find out will work.

63. Convection currents can also be established using hot and cold air. Create a replica of this experiment using air instead of water—with smoke as the indicator, instead of food coloring. Be sure to get adult supervision.

Coiling Cobra

The Experiment

A coiling cobra (not a real snake for you participants in the back seat of the performance) is a perfect way to demonstrate the movement of thermal energy by convection. A circular-shaped snake of paper is suspended above a candle or some other source of heat. The heat from the candle will create an expanding and rising convection current in the air molecules. As these air molecules expand and rise, they pass through the snake and cause it to coil and spin.

Materials

1   Piece of paper
1   Pair of scissors
1   12-inch Length of string
1   Roll of tape
1   Candle
1   Turban (optional)
1   Wooden flute (optional)
1   Large basket (optional)
   Adult supervision

Procedure

1. A review of fire safety in the lab should precede this experiment. Review the use of fire blankets, fire extinguishers (where they are and how to use them), pulling long hair back with bands, keeping loose clothing out of the way of the flame, and so on. *No horseplay on this one!*

2. Draw a circular snake on your notebook paper (see illustration on the next page). Cut along the lines.

Coiling Cobra

3. Attach a piece of string to the middle, round section of your snake with a very small piece of tape.

4. With adult supervision, light the candle. Holding onto the end of the string, place the center of the snake over the flame of the candle. The trick here is NOT to catch the paper on fire—so we would recommend a safe distance of no less than 6 inches.

5. Observe what happens to the cobra when it is exposed to the convection current created by the candle flame heating the air.

6. Safely extinguish all flames when you are done with this lab.

HOT AIR SPINS SNAKE

HOT AIR RISES

AIR HEATED

CANDLE

How Come, Huh?

The air is being heated above the candle and expanding. Thermal energy moves through the air and begins to bump into other molecules at a faster rate. The molecules move about wildly and spread out. This allows other surrounding air to push upward on the paper and spin the snake. The snake will continue to spin as long as it is held above the heat of the candle flame. Move it over to the side of the candle where it is cool, and the snake will stop spinning.

Science Fair Extensions

64. Try the following: Use a skinny snake, a fat snake, a short snake, a long snake, a heavy snake, a tissue paper snake, a plastic snake . . . that's about seven Blue Ribbon Science Fair projects right there. Collect data by counting the number of complete spins in 1 minute.

65. Let's confuse radiant energy with thermal energy. See if color will affect the number of spins? Try using white paper and black paper. Again, count the number of spins of the snake per minute.

66. Many cultures take advantage of the convection currents created by candles to create elaborate religious displays. Do some research and find out what kind of displays they are creating, what they are used for, and then adapt the designs to create a modern thermal mobile of your own.

Ring of Fire

The Experiment

In the previous experiment we saw the effect of a convection current on a paper snake. In this lab we are actually going to be able to see how the convection current moves by watching the behavior of an empty tea bag—that has been lit on fire and is burning.

The bag produces a column of hot air, and when the weight of the bag allows it to be lifted up with the rising current of hot air, you have a floating flammable tea bag. This is one of those labs that you do with an adult around—mostly, because grown-ups get a kick out of this stuff too.

Materials

1 Tea bag, paper
1 Pie tin
1 Book of matches
   Goggles (optional)
   Adult supervision

Procedure

DO THIS ACTIVITY OUT-SIDE WHERE THERE IS NO DANGER OF ANYTHING CATCHING ON FIRE. You will also want to have an **adult** around to help out.

1. Gently open the top of the tea bag and discard the contents of the bag. Open the tea bag up so that it forms a cylinder and place it in the center of the pie tin.

2. Under the supervision of an adult, light a match and touch it to the top of the tea bag in several places so that it begins to burn from the top down. Stand back and observe what happens.

How Come, Huh?

As the tea bag burned, the air directly above the bag was heated. Hot air rises, so it headed up and out leaving a vacancy. Cooler air replaced the hot air that rose toward the ceiling, and it too was heated by the burning tea bag—off to the ceiling and a convection current was created.

At a certain time in the experiment the mass of the tea bag had burned down to the point where it could be carried aloft by this current of hot air and so it lifted off the tin. Because it continued to burn as it floated, it perpetuated the convection current until all of the paper had been consumed. The ash then cooled and fell to the ground. Another mystery of nature revealed!

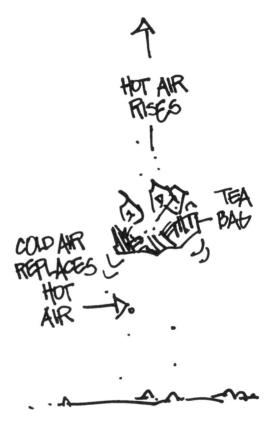

Science Fair Extensions

67. Under adult supervision, experiment with other very light papers like wrapping tissue, mimeograph separation sheets, and single-ply toilet paper. If you work it right, they all fly up into the air and produce ooh aah every time.

Convection Chimney

The Experiment

An empty, 2-liter pop bottle that has had both the top and bottom removed is placed over a lit candle. A small door has also been cut near the base of the pop bottle. A small cone of incense is lit and placed outside the pop bottle, near the door. A scarcely used Hindu ritual to summon the spirits of thermodynamics? Nope, just another way to demonstrate a convection current.

As the air inside the pop bottle is heated by the candle flame, it becomes less dense and rises. This creates an area of low pressure inside the bottle that allows cooler air to be pushed in through the opening cut at the base of the bottle. The cooler air is pushed—along with the incense, acting as a marker—into the bottle making the movement of the convection current visible to the naked eye.

Materials

1   2-liter Bottle
1   Pair of scissors
1   Candle, votive
1   Book of matches
1   Cone of incense
    Adult supervision

Procedure

1. Using the illustration on the next page, cut the top and bottom portions of the bottle off to make a plastic cylinder.

2. Cut a horseshoe shaped opening at the bottom of the cylinder approximately 1 inch wide and 2 inches high.

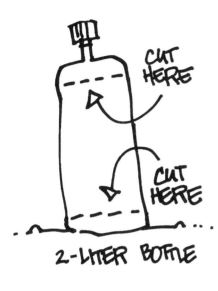

CUT HERE

CUT HERE

2-LITER BOTTLE

3. Place the candle in the middle of the table and position the cylinder over it so the candle is in the center. Place the incense just outside the door you cut in the bottom of the cylinder.

4. After observing the setup, which for the most part ranks up there with watching water evaporate, light the incense with the supervision of an adult. When it has lost its flame and begins to smolder (smoke), make observations on the action of the smoke. Allow time for observations to proceed.

5. Remove the cylinder and light the candle. Replace the cylinder, making sure the incense is near the door. All of this is pictured in the cartoon illustration found at the bottom of this page. Barring the presence of a large-scale tornado passing nearby, the smoke should head into the door, and out and up into the cylinder in the tradition of any well-behaved convection current.

SMOKE

INCENSE   CANDLE

Convection Chimney

How Come, Huh?

This setup is called a convection chimney and allows you to actually see differences in temperature between bodies of air. As the air inside the container gets warmer from the candle, it produces a column of air that is less dense than the surrounding air and it begins to rise. This leaves a vacancy inside the bottle that is quickly filled when heavier, cooler air is pushed through the door and inside the bottle. The smoke from the incense provides a visible way to see the air being pushed into the bottle, creating the convection current.

Science Fair Extensions

68. Design an experiment to test to see if a taller chimney would affect the rate that the convection current rises.

69. Fatten up the amount of heat inside the bottle. If you add more calories of heat and produce hotter, less dense air, how does that affect the experiment?

70. Create, from a shoe box and toilet paper rolls, a box with two chimneys. How could you create a convection current so air is drawn into one chimney and out the other? How would you be able to see it?

Convection Organ

The Experiment

You are going to heat with a propane torch a folded piece of metal-alloy screen stuffed into one end of a large diameter steel tube. When the torch is removed, the tube begins to hum. If you tilt the tube sideways—giving the illusion that you are "pouring" the sound out of the tube—the sound will stop. If you quickly hold the tube in a vertical position, the sound will resume.

Materials

1   Steel pipe, 19" x 1.5", with metal-alloy screen, 2" x 6"
1   Wooden dowel or hammer
1   Pair of goggles
1   Propane torch or Bunsen burner
1   Propane torch stand
1   Ignitor or book of matches
1   Oven mitt
1   Large, opaque, plastic cup
    Adult supervision

Procedure

1. These tubes are easy and relatively inexpensive to make. Head to the plumbing or hardware section of your local handyman's store, and tell them you are a science enthusiast and explain the experiment. The pipe is a section of the fence post that holds up a metal fence. The screen is a 20-gauge metal alloy that can be cut into a 2" by 6" strip, tri-folded into a 2" by 2" square, and then pounded into the bottom of the pipe using a wooden dowel and hammer.

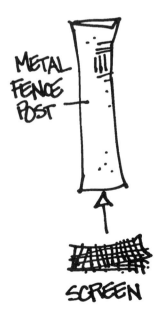

METAL
FENCE
POST

SCREEN

Convection Organ

2. With you goggles on and an adult by your side, fire up the torch and put the oven mitt on the hand that is going to hold the tube. Hate to state the apparent and obvious, but you would be surprised at some of the questions we get.

3. The key to this experiment is to get the screen inside the bottom of the tube red hot using the torch. To achieve that end, you are going to want to hold the tube upright with the metal-alloy screen toward the end nearest the torch. Use the illustration above as a guide.

4. Insert the flame of the torch into the bottom of the tube so that it is heating the alloy screen directly. When the screen gets hot enough, the tube will begin to hum, _but not until you remove the flame from inside the tube_. This usually takes about 15 to 20 seconds. Every tube is different, so it would be a good idea to practice and time your particular tube before you uncork this one on your friends.

5. At any rate, when the screen is hot enough, the tube starts to hum, eyeballs bug out, and your friends are really impressed. Don't stop now; it's zinger time. Pick up the large, opaque, plastic cup. Hold the cup up and tilt the tube at an angle, so that it looks like you are "pouring" the sound from the tube into the cup. The interesting thing is that as soon as you tip the tube over, the sound ceases.

6. Quickly return the tube to its upright position and "pour" the sound back into the tube from the cup, and it will start to hum again.

Depending on how hot you got the screen you may be able to "pour" the sound back and forth several times before the screen cools to the point where it will not produce the convection current necessary to produce the sound. As with comedy, omelettes, and good science demos, timing is everything.

How Come, Huh?

Touch a lit propane torch to anything, and it's a sure bet that it is going to get hot. As the hot screen heats the air inside the tube, a convection current starts to form and the air rises through the tube. The air escaping from the top of the tube creates an area of low pressure just above the screen, and cold air enters the bottom of the tube. As it passes through the hot screen, it is heated rapidly and starts to rise turbulently through the tube. This turbulent motion produces a wave of vibrating air molecules that our ears interpret as a hum.

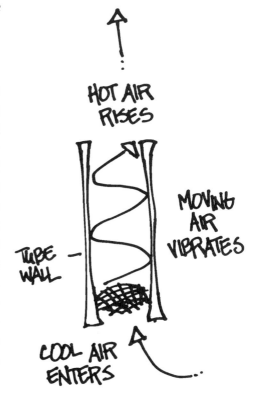

HOT AIR RISES

MOVING AIR VIBRATES

TUBE WALL

COOL AIR ENTERS

Convection Organ

When you tip the tube sideways, you disrupt the movement of the air. Because air molecules don't get a chance to bounce around inside the tube and produce the vibrations, the sound ceases. By returning the tube to its vertical position, the air is free to rise and produce sound again. For the record, you cannot pour sound. It's an illusion—that is, if it is well done. That's where the practice comes in.

Science Fair Extensions

71. Make a set of pipes using different lengths and diameters of pipe. Again, the hardware store will have a variety of different pipes, made out of different materials. Determine how these two variables affect the pitch that is produced.

72. Find out if the local church has a set of organ pipes—same concept, slightly more refined. Create an experiment that allows you to replicate a church organ pipe.

73. Propane torches throw out a lot of heat and produce a very chaotic, violent column of air. That is why you have to remove the torch before the sound becomes audible.

It is possible to produce the same kind of effect—and a much more gentle tone—using candles and tubes. Experiment, with the permission of your parents, and see if you can come up with a new musical instrument.

Big Idea 9

Heat can be conducted through solids. Solids expand when they are heated and contract when they are cooled. The amount that they change is measured as the coefficient of expansion.

Conduction Wheel

The Experiment

A conduction wheel can be purchased from one of the vendors that we list in the front of this book for about eight to ten dollars.

It looks like a six-spoked wheel without the rim. The center of the wheel is a metal disc and each of the spokes radiating out from the center is made from a different metal.

The center of the wheel is heated using a candle or alcohol burner. The heat from the flame is transferred by conduction to the rods at the same time. However, that's when the race starts.

Materials

1   Candle
1   Book of matches
5   Thumbtacks
1   Conduction wheel
1   Clock
    Adult supervision

Procedure

1. With adult supervision, light the candle and let the flame melt a small pool of wax. Extinguish the flame, dip the head of the thumbtack in the wet wax, and quickly apply it to the end of one of the spokes in the conduction wheel.

2. Repeat the procedure until you have a tack stuck to the end of each spoke of the conduction wheel.

3. Note the start time in your data table, relight the candle, and hold the center of the conduction wheel directly over the flame.

4. As the flame heats the center of the wheel, heat will be conducted down the spokes at different rates. When the metal gets hot enough, the wax will melt and the thumbtack will fall off. Note the time when each tack falls from its respective spoke.

5. The kind of metal in each spoke is identified using the symbol that has been stamped on the center disc.

Data & Observations

Metal Name	Symbol	Start	End	Time
Aluminum	A			
Steel	S			
Stainless Steel	SS			
Copper	C			
Brass	B			

How Come, Huh?

The flame of the candle heated the center disc. The center disc, in turn, heated each of the five spokes. The heat was conducted down each spoke at different speeds. The more dense the metal, the faster the heat was conducted. When the tip of the metal spoke got hot enough, the wax melted and the tack fell off.

Ring & Ball

The Experiment

When solids are heated, they expand and get larger. When they cool, they contract. A set of brass rings and spheres—easily acquired through one of the science companies listed in the front of this book for about five bucks—are used to demonstrate this point. Once in your hands, the set can be used to gather all the data necessary to demonstrate this principle using metals.

Materials

1   Set of ring and sphere
1   Propane torch
       or Bunsen burner
1   Propane torch stand
1   Ignitor or book of matches
1   Cup of ice water
1   Cup of room-temperature water
    Adult supervision

Procedure

1. While they are both cool, insert the sphere in the ring and push it on through. This is Experiment #1 in the data table to the right. Record your results in the last column as *fit* or *did not fit*.

2. Continue with all of the different combinations listed in the table until the data table is complete. Analyze the data and write a general "law" describing how heat affects metal.

Data & Observations

Expt	Ring	Sphere	Result
1	Room-Temp.	Room-Temp.	
2	Hot	Room-Temp.	
3	Hot	Ice Water	
4	Room-Temp.	Hot	
5	Ice Water	Hot	
6	Hot	Hot	
7	Ice Water	Ice Water	

How Come, Huh?

At room temperature, the diameter of the sphere and the inside diameter of the ring are very close. When the sphere is heated, it becomes too large to pass through the ring. When the ring is heated, the sphere passes through easily.

Science Fair Extensions

74. Other solids expand as well as metals. Concrete sidewalks have soft, black ribbons between the pads of concrete. Find out what would happen if they were not there.

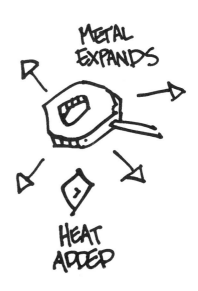

Bimetallic Strips

The Experiment

A straight, thin, metal strip made of two metals pressed together—hence the name, bimetallic—is heated in the flame of a Bunsen burner or propane torch. As the bimetallic strip absorbs the heat from the flame, it begins to expand at different rates. This demonstrates the difference in the rates (or coefficients if you want to speak phybonics) of expansion for the two different metals. Running the strip in a stream of cool water returns the strip to its original shape and also appears to have some element of magic to it.

Materials

1   Bimetallic strip
1   Propane torch
        or Bunsen burner
1   Ignitor or book of matches
        Source of running water
        Adult supervision

Procedure

1. We are going to assume that you would like to have some fun demonstrating this lab idea to your friends. Tell them that you have a special metal rod that, when heated in a flame, curves to the right.

With adult supervision, place the strip in the flame and demonstrate this idea.

2. Now to have some fun. Tell your friends that you have "polarized" water at your house. It is a kind of water that will almost immediately straighten a bent metal rod. Turn the faucet on and stick the very end of the now-curved bimetallic strip in the water and push it through slowly. As it hits the water the metal cools, contracts back to its original position, and for the uneducated eye, appears to have been straightened out by the water.

How Come, Huh?

All metals expand when they are heated, but no metals expand at the same rate. With a bimetallic strip you have two dissimilar metals pressed together. When you expose them to heat, they begin to expand— each at their own rate. The metal that expands more quickly will push the slower expanding metal to one side. That is how the rod became curved.

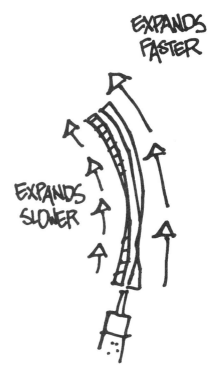

When you placed the strip in water, the metal cooled back down to room temperature and the strip was straightened out. Have fun with this one.

Science Fair Extensions

75. There is a set of lab equipment that is specifically designed to measure the expansion of metal rods in the presence of heat. It contains a dial at one end and a clamp to hold the rod in place. See if you can borrow one from the local high school physics teacher and measure the coefficient of expansion of metal rods that come with it.

Big Idea 10

Added heat can cause solids to change state and become liquids. This is called the melting point of a substance and it is used to identify the material. Added heat can also cause liquids to change state and become gases. This is called the boiling point of a substance and it is used to identify the material.

Puddle Tracing

The Experiment

This is probably one of the most basic labs in the book. Water will be sloshed on a concrete surface. Using a piece of chalk you will trace the outline of the water. After that, it is up to the sun and the laws of chemistry and physics to take over.

Materials

1   Stick of chalk
1   Bucket
1   Concrete surface
     Water
     Sun

Procedure

1. Fill the bucket with water. Go outside on a sunny, hot day and pour the water on the concrete or asphalt.

2. Using the chalk, quickly outline the puddle. Then, every 5 minutes take the chalk and trace the new outline, until the water completely evaporates.

How Come, Huh?

The chalk outline leaves a data trail of how fast the puddle evaporated (each line represents 5 minutes) and also provides evidence that the sun can provide thermal energy to cause water molecules to change from a liquid to a gas state and evaporate.

Alcohol Rub

The Experiment

Rubbing alcohol—the kind that your mom wipes on those nasty knee scrapes that you get—is very volatile. In this case, that means that it evaporates quickly in the open air.

This lab is valuable because it will go a long way to helping you understand the ideas that explain the next two labs, Drinking Bird and Hand Boiler.

The important ideas that you want to glean from this lab are that 1) liquids can change to gases quickly, easily, and with little heat, and 2) heat is absorbed in the process.

Materials

1   Bottle of isopropyl alcohol
3   Thermometers
3   Paper towels
1   Fan, electric
    Water

Procedure

1. Fold the three paper towels into quarters and insert a thermometer in each towel.

2. In a well-ventilated area, clear a table and place all three paper towel/thermometer combos in a row and put an electric fan in front of the setup.

3. Soak one paper towel in water, a second in alcohol, and leave the third one dry. Record the temperature of each towel.

4. Turn on the fan making sure that the air blows across all three towels evenly. As the air flows over the paper, it will cool the paper towels by causing some of the liquid to evaporate. Record the temperatures of all three towels every minute for 10 minutes.

Data & Observations

Time (min.)	Water	Alcohol	Dry
0			
1			
2			
3			
4			
5			
6			
7			
8			
9			
10			

Alcohol Rub

How Come, Huh?

What you should have discovered is that the towels with the water and the alcohol wound up with much lower temperatures than the towel that was dry.

The liquids absorbed heat from their surroundings—in this case, the towel—to get the energy to change the liquids to gases. The air blowing over the surface of the towels simply accelerated the process because the air moved the evaporated gas away from the surface of the towel making room for the next gas molecule. This is the reason that most folks dry off when they jump into a lake and then pop out of the water in the wind. By removing the water (via toweling off) less heat is lost.

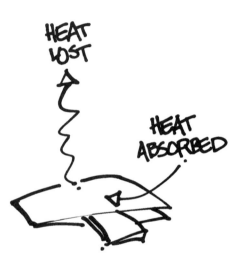

Science Fair Extensions

76. Design an experiment to demonstrate that hot liquids evaporate more quickly than cool liquids under these circumstances.

77. Rub the same amount of alcohol and water on your skin at the same time and compare the sensation that you feel. The alcohol evaporates much more quickly, so as a consequence it wicks away the heat from your body much faster.

Drinking Bird

The Experiment

The Drinking Bird has captured our imagination since the 1940s. Use the bird to generate discussion among your friends of how in blazes does it dunk over and over and over.

Materials

1   Drinking Bird
1   Glass, 10-12 oz.
    Water

Procedure

1.   Before beginning, make sure the bird's head is completely waterlogged. The fuzzy felt-like material will absorb water and plays an integral part in the action the bird makes.

2.   Place a glass full of water next to the bird, so as it dips forward toward the glass the beak dips into the water. You may have to put a small book under the bird's feet to make sure the beak reaches the water.

3.   To start the dry bird drinking all you do is simply get his head wet.

4.   Concentrate your observations on the inside of the bird's glass body. Discuss your ideas on how or why this action takes place with a friend or your mom or dad. After you have exhausted all the possibilities, come up with your own explanation before reading the answer.

Drinking Bird

How Come, Huh?

The bird is made of two evacuated glass bulbs connected by a hollow glass tube. The lower bulb contains a liquid, methylene chloride, that vaporizes very easiliy in a low-pressure environment. The head (top bulb) of the bird is covered with felt. It's probably easiest to explain this in steps. Here's how it works.

1. You dunk the bird's head in the water and get the felt wet.

2. The water in the felt starts to evaporate. To evaporate the water must steal some heat energy to change the water molecules from liquid to gas. The closest location for this heat is the bulb that the felt is covering. So, the felt steals heat energy from the bulb.

3. When the felt steals heat energy from the bulb, this lowers the temperature inside the bulb.

4. As the temperature inside the bulb is lowered, the methylene chloride vapor, which is hanging out in the top bulb, cools and turns from a gas to a liquid.

5. When a gas changes to a liquid, it takes up less space. It also lowers the pressure in the top bulb.

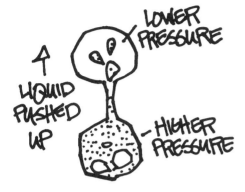

6. With the pressure lower in the top bulb there is now a difference in pressure between the top and bottom bulbs, with the bottom bulb being higher. The higher pressure in the bottom bulb pushes the liquid up into the top bulb.

7. When the liquid rushes up into the top bulb, the center of gravity is changed, making the bird top-heavy. This causes the bird to tip over and take a drink

8. When the bird is bent over drinking, a clear passage is created between the two bulbs, and the pressure inside equalizes. When this happens, the liquid runs from the top back into the bottom bulb—and the bird, with a wet head, stands back up.

9. The felt, soaking in water, starts to absorb heat energy from the top bulb and the whole cycle repeats itself.

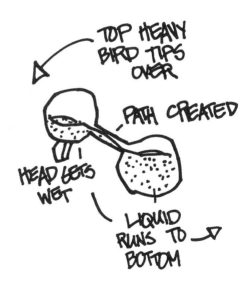

Science Fair Extensions

78. Design an experiment that proves that the temperature of the water the bird dips into makes a difference in the number of drinks per period of time.

Hand Boiler

The Experiment

A glass contraption will allow you to introduce the idea of vapor point and pressure to your friends and at the same time have a little fun with the "love meter."

Commercial hand boilers are available for a very reasonable price, usually five to eight dollars at science and novelty stores. The idea of the love meter comes in because you are supposed to hold the bottom bulb and the quicker the liquid rushes from there to the top bulb, the "hotter" the lover you are. We'll take care of that myth in a hurry.

Materials

1 Hand boiler
2 Bowls
1 Towel
   Hot water
   Ice Water
1 Hand

Procedure

1. Hold the boiler in the palm of your hand. If your hand is warm, the liquid will begin to rise to the upper bulb and bubble. Right now all we are looking for is a reference point. Note the speed with which the liquid in the bulb rushes to the upper bulb.

2. Soak the same hand in a bowl of hot water for about 30 seconds. Dry your hand and quickly place the hand boiler in the palm of your hand. Observe the speed that the liquid moves now.

3. Soak the same hand in a bowl of ice water for another 30 seconds. Dry your hand and quickly place the hand boiler in the palm of your hand. Observe the speed that the liquid moves now.

Data & Observations

Record your observations in the space provided.

1. When you held the hand boiler with your hand at your regular body temperature, was the movement of the liquid . . .

Very fast   *Fast*   *Moderate*   *Slow*   *Very Slow*

2. When you held the hand boiler with your hand after it had been in the bowl with hot water, was the movement of the liquid . . .

Very fast   *Fast*   *Moderate*   *Slow*   *Very Slow*

3. When you held the hand boiler with your hand after it had been in the bowl with cold water, was the movement of the liquid . . .

Very fast   *Fast*   *Moderate*   *Slow*   *Very Slow*

4. How would you explain the movement of the liquid inside the hand boiler based on the data that you have collected?

_____

_____

_____

_____

Hand Boiler

How Come, Huh?

When you placed your hand around the bulb at the bottom of the boiler, you increased the temperature of that bulb. Because the bulb is a fixed space, when the temperature inside the bulb goes up, pressure inside the bulb also goes up. In short, when you put your hand on the bulb, the bulb gets warmer: Molecules in the bulb get warmer, warmer molecules create more pressure inside the bulb.

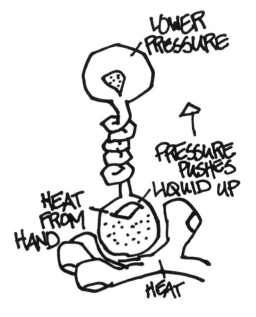

This increased pressure in the lower bulb pushes the liquid from the bottom to the top of the boiler. After all the liquid leaves, the remaining vapor continues to be heated, expands, increases the pressure in the lower bulb, and is also pushed up through the narrow tubing into the top bulb where it bubbles through the existing liquid. That's why it looks like it is boiling.

Science Fair Extensions

79. Who has the hottest hands? Conduct an experiment to see if male or female hands are warmer. Time the number of seconds it takes for the liquid to bubble when held in different hands.

80. Try placing the bulb in various temperatures of water. What does the temperature have to be before the liquid will rise?

Big Idea 11

If enough heat is added to a material that it bursts into flames, it has reached a temperature called the kindling point.

Burning Steel

The Experiment

In this experiment, you will be equipped with goggles and fire safety information. Armed with this information, attempt to melt a large steel nail over a very small flame in your desire to understand what the heck a kindling point is.

After a few attempts (you judge if you are successful or not), another type of steel (steel wool) will be placed into the flame. This is the wool of a lamb that has been living near a hard-hat construction area all of its life (just kidding, no pun intended). You will hold a piece of the steel wool (not the entire lamb) over the flame and observe that it will indeed achieve the kindling point very quickly and send out a shower of golden sparkles in celebration.

Materials

1   Pair of goggles
1   Candle, votive
1   Pie tin
1   Book of matches
1   Test tube holder
1   #16 Nail
1   00000 Steel wool pad
1   Fire blanket / fire extinguisher
Adult supervision

Procedure

1. Put goggles on and place the candle in the center of the pie tin. Ask an adult to light the candle. Use the illustration above as a guide.

2. Place the nail in the test tube holder and insert the nail into the flame of the candle. Roll the nail around inside the flame of the candle and do your very best to get it to catch on fire. After 30 seconds or so, place the HOT nail inside the pie tin. **Do NOT touch it!**

3. Take the piece of steel wool and "tease" (pull apart) the fibers into a large ball to expose the steel to plenty of oxygen—the bigger, the better. Clip one side of the ball of steel wool into the test tube holder and then place the steel wool ball in the candle flame. Use the illustration to the right as a guide.

4. The steel wool will ignite and burn and smoke. Be sure to keep holding the burning steel wool over the pie tin. When the reaction is done, release the wool from the clip and place it in the pie tin. When everything has cooled off, throw away the burned remains and keep the nail.

Data & Observations

Circle the word that best answers the question asked.

1. Which materials, steel wool or the nail, had a greater surface area exposed to the flame?

Steel Wool   Nail

2. Which materials, steel wool or the nail, were surrounded by more oxygen?

Steel Wool   Nail

Burning Steel

How Come, Huh?

This is strictly a matter of surface area. The nail will get hot but will not burn. Its mass is too large and it conducts the heat away from the flame. The steel wool is extremely fine, on the other hand, and has lots of oxygen between the fibers to help it ignite. The steel wool will reach the kindling point (the temperature when a substance bursts into flames). Did you know that the temperature that iron catches on fire (the kindling point) is actually lower than paper? The trick is getting enough oxygen to a large enough surface area to the reaction to keep it going.

Science Fair Extensions

81. You may want to experiment with different grades of steel wool. It comes in various thicknesses ranging from 00000, which is very fine, to a 5, which is not. Make sure you do not get the kind that has soap in it.

82. Try dipping the steel wool in various liquids, allowing it to dry, and then placing it in the flame. Liquids? Cola, water, juice, alcohol, soap, and so on. Use a stopwatch to record the amount of time before the wool catches on fire each time. Be sure to have an adult nearby.

Flame Jumper

The Experiment

Light a candle and let it burn for a while on the lab table. Blow out the candle. Hold a match a few centimeters above the wick and watch the flame jump from the match back down to the wick without ever touching the wick itself. Mission accomplished!

Materials

1   Candle
1   Book of matches
Adult supervision

Procedure

1. Review fire safety rules on page 17. This is important any time you or your friends are working with an open flame.

2. Have an adult light a candle. Let it burn for a few minutes until some of the wax around the wick has melted.

3. Extinguish the candle flame by licking your thumb and forefinger and then pinching the flame out. Try not to disturb or disperse the smoke by blowing the flame out.

4. Relight by holding a match a few centimeters above the wick, directly in the smoke coming from the flame. The flame will jump from the match to the wick.

Flame Jumper

How Come, Huh?

The smoke rising from the wick is made primarily of vaporized wax. This is the gas state of the wax and it is highly flammable. When you hold the match above the wick, this wax vapor is very near the kindling point of wax and catches on fire easily. Once the gas has been ignited, it will quickly ignite the rest of the vapor coming from the wick and reignite the wick itself.

It appears that the flame jumps from the match to the wick. In reality the flame from the match is lighting the wax vapor on fire—which almost instantly ignites the wick.

The other thing worth noting is that you have all three phases of wax present in this experiment. The solid wax is quite evident, as is the gas state (the smoke). If you look carefully at the base of the wick there is also a small pool of liquid wax.

Science Fair Extensions

83. Does the size of the candle affect the distance the flame will jump? Try using a large candle and a small one. Burn the candles for the same amount of time, then with adult supervision of course, put out the flame.

84. Birthday candles are great for experiments. Try this one with adult supervision. Does the color of the candle effect its burning time? Set candles in small holders of play dough. Light 4 different colors at the same time and chart minutes until the candles burn out. Repeat at least 3 times, record your data, and write your conclusions.

Big Idea 12

AND FREEZING RAIN WOULD BE ...?

Removing heat can cause gases to change state and become liquids. This is called the condensation point of a substance and it is used to identify the material. Removing heat can also cause liquids to change state and become solids. This is called the freezing point of a substance and it is used to identify the material.

Condensation Can

The Experiment

The three states of matter are solid, liquid, and gas. Most substances change from one state to another at a very predictable temperature.

A change from solid to liquid is called the melting point. A change from liquid to solid is called the freezing point. They are identical. Changes from liquid to gas or from gas to liquid are called the vaporization or condensation points, respectively, and they are also the same.

This lab will allow you to observe, measure, and record the temperature of three states of water and the transition points between those changes.

Materials

1   1000-ml Beaker or quart saucepan
   Ice cubes
   Water
1   C° Thermometer
1   Hot plate or stove
1   Clock
1   Metal soup can, #303
   Adult supervision

Procedure

1. Fill the beaker half full with ice cubes and then add water to the level of the ice cubes. Insert the thermometer, gently swirl it around a couple of times and record the temperature on the 0 line of the Temp. column of the data table on the next page.

2. With an adult nearby, turn the hot plate or stove on and record the temperature for every minute in the spaces provided in the data table below. Continue to heat the ice water mixture until the water has boiled for three minutes or more.

3. Once you have observed the transitions from solid to liquid to gas and recorded the temperatures in the table below, graph the data that you collected on a separate sheet of paper.

Data & Observations

Time (min.)	Temp. (°C)	Time (min.)	Temp. (°C)
0		11	
1		12	
2		13	
3		14	
4		15	
5		16	
6		17	
7		18	
8		19	
9		20	
10			

Condensation Can

4. To continue the process of exploring states of matter take a metal soup can and fill it with ice cubes; then add water until the can is full. Place a thermometer in the can and record the temperature of the water on a separate sheet of paper.

5. Place the can in a warm spot and observe what happens to the outer sides of the can. Record the temperature of the water when you start to see drops of water forming on the outside of the can. This water appears on the outside of the can because water in the air, called vapor, comes in contact with the cold surface of the can and condenses there. The same process creates clouds in the sky.

How Come, Huh?

When you graphed out the data, you should have noticed that the temperature of the ice water did not change very much as the ice was melting. This is represented by a fairly flat line starting out your graph.

Once all of the ice had melted and changed to liquid water, the temperature started to rise. It continued to rise until the water approached the boiling point.

As the water started to boil, the graphing line once again leveled off meaning that the temperature of the solution remained the same. This is how chemists identify the transition points of different compounds. Once the temperature line levels off, the transition point has been reached.

Science Fair Extensions

85. Experiment with recording and determining the melting point of several soft solids, like butter, lard, or Crisco.

86. Experiment with recording and determining the boiling point of several liquids of your choice. Be sure to have an adult approve your choices—stay away from flammable liquids.

Swiss Cheese Candles

The Experiment

Making your own candles and taking advantage of the states of matter will create some fun investigations of matter. When hot, liquid wax is poured into a container filled with ice cubes, the ice will take up space and the wax will harden into interesting shapes. Add a wick and voila! you have created a unique, one-of-a-kind, Swiss cheese candle. Add a gift tag and you may put a smile on someone's face for a special gift occasion.

Materials

- 1   Electric skillet
-     Water
- 1   Metal soup can, #303
- 1   Cube of paraffin
-     Crayon pieces
- 1   Small wax cup
- 1   Heavy cotton string
- 1   Ice cubes
- 1   Oven mitt

Procedure

1. With the supervision of an adult, plug the electric skillet into the wall and adjust the setting to medium high. Keep in mind that every skillet will be a little different so feel free to adjust the temperature. Add enough water to fill the bottom of the pan about one-half-inch deep.

SC Candles

2. Place the soup can in the heating water and add chunks of paraffin wax to the can as well as pieces of colored crayon if you are looking to add some zing to your final product.

3. Take the wax cup and place one end of the cotton string in the bottom. Add a couple of ice cubes and wind the string around them. Add a couple of more ice cubes, each time wiggling the string in and around the cubes. You should have at least 1 inch of string, more is fine, left over when you fill the carton full of ice cubes.

4. Put the oven mitt on and remove the can of melted paraffin from the electric skillet. Pour paraffin into the wax cup and over the ice cubes. The wax will almost immediately set up and solidify, but you are going to want to leave the wax cup sitting overnight so that eventually all of the ice will melt.

5. The next day you can pour off the water from the melted ice cubes. Carefully tear the paper of the wax cup from the candle, and you will be able to see where the ice cubes were once present.

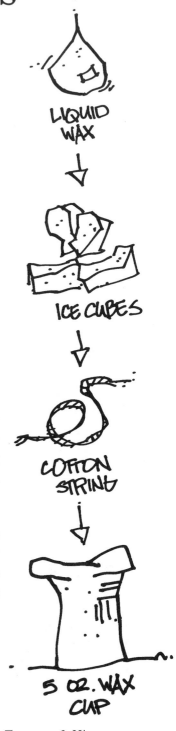

LIQUID WAX

ICE CUBES

COTTON STRING

5 OZ. WAX CUP

6. If you time this just right, you have your Christmas present, Mother's or Father's Day gift, or simply a fun table decoration for Cheese Day, of which there has got be a least one, especially if you live in Wisconsin.

How Come, Huh?

There are three important ideas at work here: 1) Matter can be defined as anything that takes up space and has mass. Frozen water (ice) takes up space and has mass. 2) No two kinds of matter can occupy the same space at the same time. When hot wax is poured over the ice cubes, the wax takes the shape of the container and surrounds the ice. 3) When liquids change to solids, it is because they have reached their freezing point. So, when the wax hit the ice, it froze or hardened.

Eventually the ice melted, bubbles of empty space were formed, creating a "Swiss cheese" candle.

Science Fair Extensions

87. The same kind of process creates what are called casts. These are fossils that get coated in volcanic ash, sediment, or some other casting materials; and when the original fossil decomposes, impressions of the fossil are left behind. Create a lab to demonstrate this idea.

Ice Cube Fishing

The Experiment

Sometimes the temperature of a substance can be affected by things other than heat. When two chemicals are mixed together and they absorb heat from their surroundings, they are called *endothermic*; but if they produce heat, they are called *exothermic*.

In this lab, salt will be added to water, causing it to refreeze. We are going to take advantage of this reaction to capture a couple of wayward ice cubes. Using nothing more than a piece of cotton string and a little chemistry savvy.

Materials

1   Ice cube
1   Length of string, 12 inches-18 inches
1   Packet of salt
1   5-inch Diameter pie tin

Procedure

1. Rinse the ice cube under the water for just a second and then place it in the pie tin. Place the string directly on top of the ice cube. Do your very best to catch it. Wrap it under, around, speak with it sternly if you must, but no touching.

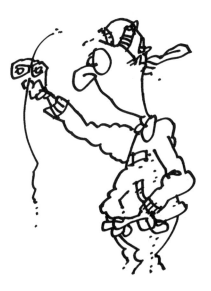

2. When your frustration level is tapped out, open the salt packet, lay the string across the top of the ice cube, and sprinkle a little bit of salt over the surface of the ice cube. Be sure to sprinkle salt on the string as well.

3. Count to five and lift the loose end of the string—and you too can be an accomplished ice-cube fisherman.

4. Once you have caught one ice cube, go for the record. Lay as many ice cubes together as your supply will allow. Then wiggle the string in around and through the assortment, and salt the entire collection. As you do this, you may want to be careful when you salt—some folks have a special ability to get the ice cubes to freeze to the pie tin.

5. As your string grows, see if you can get ice cubes that you have already caught to catch other ice cubes even without the string coming in direct contact with them.

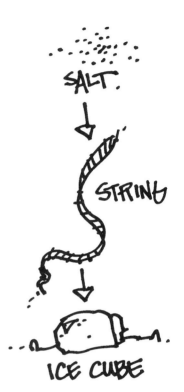

How Come, Huh?

As the ice cube sits at room temperature, it begins to melt, and a layer of water is formed on the surface of the cube. When you place the string on the ice cube, nothing happens, but it does get slightly wet in the water layer.

The salt lowers the melting point of the water (ice), which allows more of the ice to melt. The temperature of the ice lowers to its new melting point. As the water runs off the ice cube, it carries away the dissolved salt and this causes the melting point to return to its old home of 32°F. The ice is still colder than the 32°F so some of the water in the string freezes to the ice cube, and you are able to rescue the ice cube from the table.

Ice Cube Fishing

Science Fair Extensions

88. With the help of an adult, substitute dry ice for regular ice. Do you need salt? Do you need water? How could a lab like this be completed? What safety precautions would you need to take using dry ice?

89. This is not so much an extension of science as a fun activity that you can do with your friends—have an ice-cube relay. Give each kid a cotton string and line them up in two lines at one end of the competition area. Have a pile of ice cubes at the other end. When the starter says, "Go," the kids race down to the pile of ice cubes, line up and salt as many of them as possible, and race back to the line. The team with the most ice cubes wins.

90. There are several commercial brands of ice melter available on the market. These are chemicals that folks spread on their sidewalks and driveways to remove snow and ice. Try these and see if there is a successful alternative to table salt.

91. Experiment with different types of string. Or, if you are feeling somewhat adventurous and impervious to the potential failures, use different kinds of line: picture wire, fishing line, welding rods, and anything that dribbles from your imagination.

92. Does the same thing work with crushed ice? How about a snow cone? Inquiring minds want to know.

Big Idea 13

SOLID DIRECTLY TO A GAS? SOUNDS LIKE YOU'RE EATIN' MEXICAN TO ME.

Some materials change directly from solids to gases or from gases to solids. This characteristic is called sublimation.

Caffeine Crystal Vapor

The Experiment

Most substances change state one step at a time. If they are solids, they melt and become liquids; and once liquids, they change to a gas if there is enough heat. Occasionally, you get a material that is in a big hurry and sublimates, or goes directly from a solid to a gas without taking time to become a liquid. Caffeine is one such substance.

You are going to take pure, white caffeine powder and heat it in a test tube. The solid will turn directly to a vapor and then the vapor will recondense on the bottom of a second tube without ever becoming a liquid at any time during the process.

Materials

1   Vial of caffeine powder
1   Craft stick
1   20mm by 150mm Test tube
1   16mm by 150mm Test tube
1   Candle, votive
1   Magnifying lens
1   Book of matches
Adult supervison

Procedure

1. Place a small scoop of caffeine in the larger of the two test tubes. A small scoop being defined as much as you can get to stay on the end of a craft stick.

2. Insert the smaller test tube into the larger one until it is about an inch above the caffeine crystals. There is an illustration on the next page that shows you how to hold the two tubes.

3. Hold the 2 test tubes over a candle flame for about 3 to 4 minutes. You should see the caffeine start to disappear, then begin to condense on the smaller test tube in the form of fine, white, needle-like crystals.

4. Carefully remove the smaller test tube and observe the newly formed crystals with a magnifying lens.

CAFFEINE

How Come, Huh?

The states of matter are solid, liquid, and gas. When the caffeine is heated in the large test tube, it will become a gas without passing through the liquid phase. The gas will then come in contact with the bottom of the smaller test tube and condense on it without going through the gas phase.

Science Fair Extensions

93. This is another variation on observing the states of matter. THIS ONE REQUIRES GOGGLES AND ADULT SUPERVISION!! Cut the stem off of a small pipette so that only a stub remains. Smash up some dry ice to powder form and carefully scoop it into the end of the pipette. When you have the bottom of the pipette bulb covered with dry ice, fold the stub of the pipette over a couple of times and hold onto it with a pair of pliers. In a matter of seconds, the dry ice will begin to melt and you will see some liquid in the bottom of the pipette. Remember, dry ice is famous for sublimation, so this liquid state is unusual to see. Very quickly, the ice will continue to sublimate and the little bulb on the end will fill with gas and BLOW with a very loud pop.

Old Foggy Top

The Experiment

This experiment uses the interest-catching effects of dry ice to study sublimation. Squirt a little dish liquid into a glass full of water. Drop in a few pieces of dry ice and watch the bubble parade begin. A bubble parade is a continuous stream of bubbles flowing out of the glass that migrate down the side and sometimes even onto the table.

Materials

1   12-oz. Drinking glass or Toobe
1   12-inch Pie tin
1   Bottle of liquid soap
1   Spoon
1   Piece of dry ice
1   Pair of cotton gloves
    Water
    Adult supervision

Procedure

1. With an adult, review all safety rules concerning the handling of dry ice. Dry ice is usually around 112 degrees Fahrenheit below zero. What this means is that it will instantly freeze any moisture on your skin as well as the liquid in the cells in your skin. This can cause a "cold burn," also known as frost. Never pick up dry ice with your bare hands or put any near or in your mouth.

2. Fill the Toobe or glass almost full with water. Leave about 5 centimeters of space from the top. Place the Toobe in the middle of a pie tin to catch any spills. Squirt a small amount of liquid soap into the water. Insert the spoon and mix the soap and the water thoroughly.

3. Put on the gloves and using the same spoon, gently drop a chunk of dry ice the size of a Ping-Pong ball into the water and observe what happens.

4. More dry ice and soap may be added as the reaction slows down.

How Come, Huh?

Dry ice is actually solid carbon dioxide gas that has been manufactured under great pressure. When the ice is exposed to the air, the frozen gas sublimates. *Sublimate* is a term that means that the compound goes directly from a solid state to a gas state without pausing and taking time to be a liquid. If you look at the chunk of dry ice at the bottom of your Toobe, you can see the gas rushing to escape from the dry ice.

All of this frozen, very compact gas is being released into the water and rises to the top of the Toobe. As it migrates there, it does not have a whole lot of time to warm up; so when it reaches the surface of the water, it immediately comes in contact with the warm, moist air in the room. Fog forms instantly when the two gases meet. The soap in the solution traps the gas and bubbles begin to form. As more gas is released, it starts to push the gas that was first released out of the Toobe and the parade is under way!

DRY ICE

SOAP

WATER

TOOBE

Old Foggy Top

Science Fair Extensions

There are quite a few experiments that can be done with dry ice with adult supervision. In every instance the dry ice is undergoing a constant state of sublimation. Have fun!

94. Create a design for the top of the Toobe that produces different shapes of bubbles and, in effect, alters the appearance of the parade.

95. Put a small piece of dry ice in a test tube and place a balloon over the mouth of the test tube. As the dry ice sublimates, the tube will fill with gas, and eventually the balloon will fill with carbon dioxide.

96. Place a small piece of dry ice in a test tube and place a solid, rubber stopper over the test tube. As the dry ice sublimates, the pressure will continue to increase to the point where the stopper will shoot out of the test tube like a cannonball.

97. Fill an aquarium with pieces of dry ice. Blow soap bubbles so that they float over and land in the aquarium. If you wait two or three minutes, the aquarium will be filled with dry ice, and the bubbles—being less dense—will appear to be floating in midair.

98. Pack a hot dog in dry ice and leave it there for several minutes. Pull it out with tongs and drop it on a hard surface. It will have crystallized, so when it hits the ground it will shatter.

Big Idea 14

Heat causes the molecules in some materials to rearrange. When this happens, a measurable change can be observed.

Scambled Attraction

The Experiment

This lab, inspired by the Exploratorium Science Snacks series, starts out the experiments for Big Idea 14. A magnet is normally attracted to a piece of iron. If an iron wire gets too hot—called the Curie point, the wire loses its ability to be magnetized.

Materials

1   Box of Tinkertoys
1   Donut magnet
1   12-inch Piece of cotton string
1   12-inch Piece of single-strand, iron wire
2   Alligator clips
1   6-Volt lantern battery
1   Clock with sweep second hand or stopwatch
1   12-inch Piece of double-strand, iron wire
1   12-inch Piece of triple-strand, iron wire

Procedure

1. Using four wheels and six wooden posts from your pile of Tinkertoys, build the setup that is pictured in the upper right-hand portion of the next page. Or, if you choose, a wire hanger bent into a similar shape will also work nicely.

2. Tie one end of the string to the top wood post marked *A* and tie the other end of the string to the donut magnet.

3. Wrap the single-strand piece of iron wire between posts *B* and *C*.

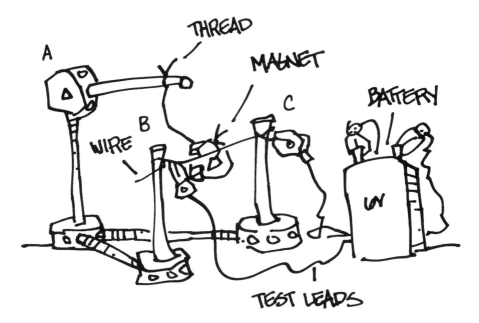

4. Move the magnet so that it comes in contact with the iron wire and sticks to it. If there is a lot of slack in the wire, wrap the other end of the string around the wood post so that it looks like the drawing above.

5. Attach one alligator lead to each post and the positive lead to the iron wire. Do not connect the other lead until you are ready to time the experiment.

6. Note the beginning time in the Data & Observations section and attach the second alligator lead to the iron wire. As the electricity flows, the wire will heat up. When it heats to the point where it loses its ability to produce a magnetic field—the Curie point, the magnet will release from the wire and swing freely. When this happens, record the time.

7. Let the wire cool and you will notice that the magnet will stick to it once again.

Scambled Attraction

8. Replace the single-strand wire with the double-strand wire and repeat the experiment again. Record the time and repeat the experiment with the triple-strand wire.

Data & Observations

# Strands	Beginning Time	Ending Time	Actual Time
1			
2			
3			

How Come, Huh?

As the iron particles in the wire get hotter and hotter, they start to wiggle around. The wire expands, everything loosens up. When this happens the atoms lose their ability to line up, work together, and form a magnetic field. They get scrambled. The magnet releases from the wire when the temperature gets hot enough, and no magnetic field is produced. When the wire cools down, the atoms can once again realign and will again attract the magnet.

Science Fair Extensions

99. Experiment with a single strand of wire but change the distance between the leads. Graph your data and explain why the times change.

100. Repeat the experiment but substitute copper wire.

Light-Sensitive Beads

The Experiment

This activity will make you look like the David Copperfield of light and color in the eyes of your friends. You are going to make the invisible visible. Ultraviolet waves are really out there. If you don't believe it, lie outside all day long some hot, sunny July day in your little bikini without sunblock and then immerse yourself in a tub of hot water that same evening. What a wonderful sensation that is! You are feeling the effects of ultraviolet waves on your damaged skin cells—not to mention the added benefit of looking like a lobster with a little white bathing suit painted on.

The first part of this activity is simply to observe a color change that occurs when the beads absorb ultraviolet light and then radiate visible light. The lab suggests testing the effects of using a sunblock on the beads.

Materials

5 Ultraviolet beads
1 Pipe cleaner
1 Egg carton
1 Piece of clear, plastic wrap

1 Roll of masking tape
1 Pair of scissors
1 Bottle of sunblock
1 Sun (free from dawn until dusk!)

Procedure

1. String the five beads on the pipe cleaner and record the color of each bead, from 1 to 5, in the space provided on the next page.

2. Now, wear the pipe cleaner on your wrist, ankle, toe, or ear and quietly exit outside into the bright sunshine, taking this book and a pencil with you. Record your observations in the data table.

Light-Sensitive Beads

3. Prepare your egg carton by cutting a two-egg section from the bottom half of the tray. Take the beads off of the pipe cleaner and place two to three beads in each section of your egg carton. Put a piece of clear plastic wrap over one egg section and leave the other open.

4. Head outside once again and expose your beads to the sun. Record observations below.

5. At this time, and with the permission of your folks, you may want to continue exploring the light-blocking abilities by using fabrics, colored paper, different strengths of sunblock, or sunglass lenses.

Data & Observations

Bead #	Color Indoors	Color Outdoors
1		
2		
3		
4		
5		

Bead #	Uncovered	Covered in Plastic
1		
2		
3		
4		
5		

How Come, Huh?

Ultraviolet waves are produced by all stars, including our Sun. This light is transmitted through electromagnetic waves, which means that they are measurable waves, usually 0.28 microns to 0.40 microns. The longer waves are generally attributed to causing the production of melanin and a nice tan; the shorter ones rip right through the cells and cream the nuclei. We call that cancer if it gets out of hand.

The ultraviolet beads used in this experiment contain a pigment that absorbs the ultraviolet light from the sun and then radiates it back to us as visible light. The way we think this happens is illustrated to the right and on page 178.

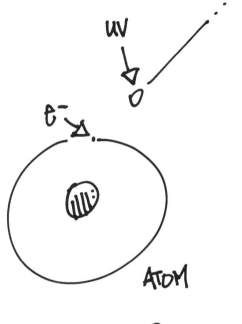

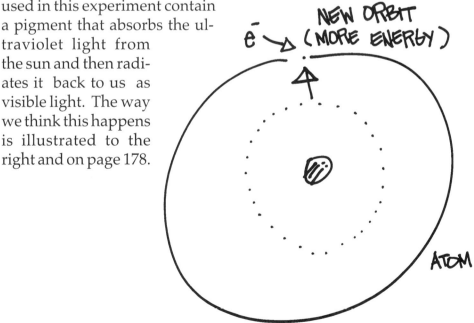

Light-Sensitive Beads

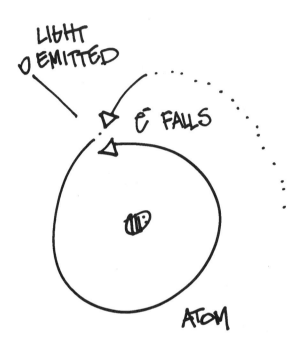

LIGHT EMITTED

e̅ FALLS

ATOM

1. A photon of UV light zips away from the Sun, travels 93,000,000 miles in about eight minutes, and zips through our atmosphere dodging numerous obstacles to smash into the pigment, which happens to be a molecule, embedded in the bead. You have just added energy to the molecule so something has to change. In this case . . .

2. The collision bumps one of the electrons (illustrated as e-) in the molecule from its regular, comfortable orbit to one that is a little bit farther away from the center of the atom. Translation: The energy from the light was absorbed by and stored in the electron's orbit, until . . .

3. This creates an unstable situation, and the electron—wanting to get rid of this extra energy—emits it as light that we see and then returns to its regular orbit, where it continues to hover comfortably around the nucleus . . . until the next UV particle creams the electrons again. This bumps an unsuspecting electron into a new orbit . . . and so it goes.

Science Fair Extensions

101. Experiment with different sources of UV light. In addition to the sun try tanning beds, food-heating lamps, various lightbulbs, and UV lamps. Rate the amount of color change and determine how juiced each of these sources are.

102. Repeat the experiment using different brands of sunglasses. Check the glasses that are for sale in the store. Many of them claim that they block harmful UV rays. Place the UV beads in egg cartons and place the sunglass lens over each bead. Record the amount of the color change for each lens and rate them for their effectiveness.

103. Place the beads in the egg carton again and this time cover them with different materials such as black fabric, cellophane, wax paper, aluminum foil, and anything else you can think of to potentially block the UV rays. Record the color changes for each material.

104. The company that manufactures these beads also produces UV-sensitive nail polish that changes colors in the sunlight. Design an experiment that uses UV-sensitive nail polish.

Memory Wire

The Experiment

Memory wire is the commercial name for a metal alloy made up of nickel and titanium called Nitinol. We tossed this in here at the very end of the book because it is a metal that has unique properties. Instead of expanding when heated, it contracts, but even more interesting is that a particular shape can be set in a high-temperature furnace that the wire "remembers." Take the wire and bend it into loops, corners, and funny shapes, then hold it over a candle flame, and the wire contracts and "remembers" the original shape.

Materials

1   6-inch Piece of memory wire
1   Bowl
    Hot water
1   Candle, votive
1   Book of matches
1   Battery with holder
2   Alligator clips
    Adult supervision

Procedure

1. Take a piece of memory wire and bend it into any kind of funny shape that you would like. Plunk the design in a bowl of hot water and watch it return to its original shape.

2. Bend it again but this time with adult supervision apply heat in the form of a candle flame that you wave back and forth under the wire.

3. And for your grand finale, bend it one more time, hook an alligator clip to each end of the wire and connect it to a battery. As the electricity flows through the wire, it generates heat. This heat is sufficient enough to cause the wire to remember its original shape so it will slowly unwind and become straight once again.

How Come, Huh?

This kind of metal alloy has two distinct phases that are determined by temperature. When you bend the metal at room temperature, it is kind of like setting a mouse trap. You bend the metal (set the trap), but with the addition of more energy (heat), the crystals in the metal spring back to their original shape—it's a slow spring that could better be classified as unwinding. In either case, it is the addition of heat that triggers the change in shape and return to the original position (straight).

That's it, 50 labs under your belt. Hope you had fun! Take a short break and we hope to see you again soon!

Science Fair Projects

•

A Step-by-Step Guide: From Idea To Presentation

Science Fair Projects

Ah, the impending science fair project—a good science fair project has the following five characteristics:

1. The student must come up with an *original* question.
2. That *original* question must be suited to an experiment in order to provide an answer.
3. The *original* idea is outlined with just one variable isolated.
4. The *original* experiment is performed and documented using the scientific method.
5. A presentation of the *original* idea in the form of a lab write-up and display board is completed.

Science Fair Projects

As simple as science fair versus science project sounds, it gets screwed up millions of times a year by sweet, unsuspecting students who are counseled by sweet, unknowing, and probably just as confused parents.

To give you a sense of contrast we have provided a list of legitimate science fair projects and then reports that do not qualify. We will also add some comments in italics that should help clarify why they do or do not qualify in the science fair project department.

Science Fair Projects

1. Temperature and the amount of time it takes mealworms to change to beetles.

Great start. We have chosen a single variable that is easy to measure: temperature. From this point forward the student can read, explore, and formulate an original question that is the foundation for the project.

A colleague of mine actually did a similar type of experiment for his master's degree. His topic: The rate of development of fly larva in cow poop as a function of temperature. No kidding. He found out that the warmer the temperature of the poop the faster the larva developed into flies.

2. The effect of different concentrations of soapy water on seed germination.

Again, wonderful. Measuring the concentration of soapy water. This leads naturally into original questions and a good project.

3. Crystal size and the amount of sugar in the solution.

This could lead into other factors such as exploring the temperature of the solution, the size of the solution container, and other variables that may affect crystal growth. Opens a lot of doors.

vs. Science Reports

4. Helicopter rotor size and the speed at which it falls.

Size also means surface area, which is very easy to measure. The student who did this not only found the mathematical threshold with relationship to air friction, but she had a ton of fun.

5. The ideal ratio of baking soda to vinegar to make a fire extinguisher.

Another great start. Easy to measure and track, leads to a logical question that can either be supported or refuted with the data.

Each of those topics *measures* one thing such as the amount of sugar, the concentration of soapy water, or the ideal size. If you start with an idea that allows you to measure something, then you can change it, ask questions, explore, and ultimately make a *prediction*, also called a *hypothesis*, and experiment to find out if you are correct. Here are some well-meaning but misguided entries:

Science Reports, <u>not Projects</u>
1. Dinosaurs!

OK, great. Everyone loves dinosaurs but where is the experiment? Did you find a new dinosaur? Is Jurassic Park alive and well, and we are headed there to breed, drug, or in some way test them? Probably not. This was a report on T. rex. Cool, but not a science fair project. And judging by the protest that this kid's mom put up when the kid didn't get his usual "A", it is a safe bet that she put a lot of time in and shared in the disappointment.

More Reports &

2. Our Friend the Sun
Another very large topic, no pun intended. This could be a great topic. Sunlight is fascinating. It can be split, polarized, reflected, refracted, measured, collected, converted. However, this poor kid simply chose to write about the size of the sun, regurgitating facts about its features, cycles, and other astrofacts while simultaneously offending the American Melanoma Survivors Society. Just kidding about that last part.

3. Smokers' Poll
A lot of folks think that they are headed in the right direction here. Again, it depends on how the kid attacks the idea. Are they going to single out race? Heredity? Shoe size? What exactly are they after here? The young lady who did this report chose to make it more of a psychology-studies effort than a scientific report. She wanted to know family income, if they fought with their parents, how much stress was on the job, and so on. All legitimate concerns but not placed in the right slot.

4. The Majestic Moose
If you went out and caught the moose, drugged it to see the side effects for disease control, or even mated it with an elk to determine if you could create an animal that would become the spokesanimal for the Alabama Dairy Farmers' Got Melk? promotion, that would be fine. But, another fact-filled report should be filed with the English teacher.

5. How Tadpoles Change into Frogs
Great start, but they forgot to finish the statement. We know how tadpoles change into frogs. What we don't know is how tadpoles change into frogs if they are in an altered environment, if they are hatched out of cycle, if they are stuck under the tire of an off-road vehicle blatantly driving through a protected wetland area. That's what we want to know. How tadpoles change into frogs, if, when, or under what measurable circumstances.

Now that we have beat the chicken squat out of this introduction, we are going to show you how to pick a topic that can be adapted to become a successful science fair project after one more thought.

One Final Comment

A Gentle Reminder

Quite often I discuss the scientific method with moms and dads, teachers and kids, and get the impression that, according to their understanding, there is one, and only one, scientific method. This is not necessarily true. There are lots of ways to investigate the world we live in and on.

Paleontologists dig up dead animals and plants but have no way to conduct experiments on them. They're dead. Albert Einstein, the most famous scientist of the last century and probably on everybody's starting five of all time, never did experiments. He was a theoretical physicist, which means that he came up with a hypothesis, skipped over collecting materials for things like black holes and space-time continuums, didn't experiment on anything or even collect data. He just went straight from hypothesis to conclusion, and he's still considered part of the scientific community. You'll probably follow the six steps we outline but keep an open mind.

Project Planner

This outline is designed to give you a specific set of time lines to follow as you develop your science fair project. Most teachers will give you 8 to 11 weeks notice for this kind of assignment. We are going to operate from the shorter time line with our suggested schedule, which means that the first thing you need to do is get a calendar.

A. The suggested time to be devoted to each item is listed in parentheses next to that item. Enter the date of the Science Fair and then, using the calendar, work backward entering dates.

B. As you complete each item, enter the date that you completed it in the column between the goal (due date) and project item.

Goal	Completed	Project Item

1. Generate a Hypothesis (2 weeks)

_____	_____	Review Idea Section, pp. 191–198
_____	_____	Try Several Experiments
_____	_____	Hypothesis Generated
_____	_____	Finished Hypothesis Submitted
_____	_____	Hypothesis Approved

2. Gather Background Information (1 week)

_____	_____	Concepts / Discoveries Written Up
_____	_____	Vocabulary / Glossary Completed
_____	_____	Famous Scientists in Field

& Time Line

Goal   Completed   Project Item

3. Design an Experiment (1 week)

————   ————   Procedure Written
————   ————   Lab Safety Review Completed
————   ————   Procedure Approved
————   ————   Data Tables Prepared
————   ————   Materials List Completed
————   ————   Materials Acquired

4. Perform the Experiment (2 weeks)

————   ————   Scheduled Lab Time

5. Collect and Record Experimental Data (part of 4)

————   ————   Data Tables Completed
————   ————   Graphs Completed
————   ————   Other Data Collected and Prepared

6. Present Your Findings (2 weeks)

————   ————   Rough Draft of Paper Completed
————   ————   Proofreading Completed
————   ————   Final Report Completed
————   ————   Display Completed
————   ————   Oral Report Outlined on Index Cards
————   ————   Practice Presentation of Oral Report
————   ————   Oral Report Presentation
————   ————   Science Fair Setup
————   ————   Show Time!

Scientific Method
· Step 1 ·
The Hypothesis

The Hypothesis

A hypothesis is an educated guess. It is a statement of what you think will probably happen. It is also the most important part of your science fair project because it directs the entire process. It determines what you study, the materials you will need, and how the experiment will be designed, carried out, and evaluated. Needless to say, you need to put some thought into this part.

There are four steps to generating a hypothesis:

Step One • Pick a Topic
Preferably something that you are interested in studying. We would like to politely recommend that you take a peek at physical science ideas (physics and chemistry) if you are a rookie and this is one of your first shots at a science fair project. These kinds of lab ideas allow you to repeat experiments quickly. There is a lot of data that can be collected, and there is a huge variety to choose from.

If you are having trouble finding an idea, all you have to do is pick up a compilation of science activities (like this one) and start thumbing through it. Go to the local library or head to a bookstore and you will find a wide and ever-changing selection to choose from. Find a topic that interests you and start reading. At some point an idea will catch your eye, and you will be off to the races.

Pick a Topic . . .

We hope you find an idea you like between the covers of this book. But we also realize that 1) there are more ideas about heat than we have included in this book and 2) other kinds of presentations, or methods of writing labs, may be just what you need to trigger a new idea or put a different spin on things. So, without further adieu, we introduce you to several additional titles that may be of help to you in developing a science fair project.

For Older Kids . . .

1. Molecules and Heat. Written by Robert Friedhoffer ISBN 0-531-11053-2 Published by Franklin Watts. 112 pages.

Part of the very entertaining Scientific Magic series. This book was the most fun to read of all that I found in the library. It starts with the simplest ideas and builds concepts until they are more difficult. Along the way you learn about the history of the thermometer, heat, and how things came to be. Not only that but after you do the experiments, there are challenges, called Bechas, and magic tricks that tie to the physics ideas that you are learning. Toss in a bunch of riddles, some silly jokes to tell while you are performing, and you can have lot of fun learning about heat. I did.

2. Heat FUNdamentals: Funtastic Science Experiments for Kids. Written by Robert W. Wood. ISBN 0-7910-4842-x Published by Chelsea House, Inc. 126 pages.

Thirty-one lab activities are presented in a fun and entertaining manner. The labs are on the elementary end of the scale for difficulty, using common household materials for virtually every lab. The steps are illustrated with cartoons and every lab has several fun facts for kids to commit to memory. There is a glossary and index at the end. This book is a part of a series of physics books for kids. Check other physics books we have written and you will find more of Mr. Wood's books recommended in this same section.

Find an Idea You Like

3. Science Projects About Science and Heat. Written by Robert Gardner and Eric Kemer. ISBN 1-89490-534-1 Published by Enslow. 126 pages.

Saying there are twenty-four labs in seven chapters is deceiving because each lab has several extensions and additional ideas for you to try. The book is written for older kids who have a good grasp of math skills. Mr. Gardner introduces simple formulas to calculate specific heat, calorie content, and coefficient of expansion in metals for starters. Great book for advanced students.

4. Heat and Cold. Written by Peter Lafferty. ISBN 0-7614-0033-8 Published by Benchmark Books. 64 pages.

A very engaging book for kids. Topics are covered in five chapters that each have several hands-on science experiments per chapter. Very good illustrations and photos support the ideas that are being presented. Text is interspersed with fun facts, definitions of words, and graphs and illustrations.

For Younger Kids . . .

5. Temperature and You. Written by Betsy and Giulio Maestro. ISBN 0-525-67271-0 Published by Lodestar Books. 32 pages.

A great book for younger kids. Several hands-on lab activities guide you through the basic ideas on heat, thermometers, and temperature. Entertaining illustrations, wonderful introduction for young scientists.

6. Hot and Cold by Karen Bryant-Mole. ISBN 1-57572-628-9 Published by Heinenmann Interactive Library. 24 pages.

A very basic introduction to temperature. Geared for very young students—building their vocabulary and basic experiences.

Develop an Original Idea

Step Two • Do the Lab

Choose a lab activity that looks interesting and try the experiment. Some kids make the mistake of thinking that all you have to do is find a lab in a book, repeat the lab, and you are on the gravy train with biscuit wheels. Your goal is to ask an ORIGINAL question, not repeat an experiment that has been done a bazillion times before.

As you do the lab, be thinking not only about the data you are collecting, but of ways you could adapt or change the experiment to find out new information. The point of the science fair project is to have you become an actual scientist and contribute a little bit of new knowledge to the world.

You know that they don't pay all of those engineers good money to sit around and repeat other people's lab work. The company wants new ideas so if you are able to generate and explore new ideas you become very valuable, not only to that company but to society. It is the question-askers that find cures for diseases, create new materials, figure out ways to make existing machines energy efficient, and change the way that we live. For the purpose of illustration, we are going to take a lab titled, "Prisms, Water Prisms." from another book, *Photon U*, and run it through the rest of the process. The lab uses a tub of water, an ordinary mirror, and light to create a prism that splits the light into the spectrum of a rainbow. Cool. Easy to do. Not expensive and open to all kinds of adaptations, including the four that we discuss on the next page.

Step Three • *Bend, Fold, Spindle, & Mutilate Your Lab*
Once you have picked out an experiment, ask if it is possible to do any of the following things to modify it into an original experiment. You want to try and change the experiment to make it more interesting and find out one new, small piece of information.

Heat it	Freeze it	Reverse it	Double it
Bend it	Invert it	Poison it	Dehydrate it
Drown it	Stretch it	Fold it	Ignite it
Split it	Irradiate it	Oxidize it	Reduce it
Chill it	Speed it up	Color it	Grease it
Expand it	Substitute it	Remove it	Slow it down

If you take a look at our examples, that's exactly what we did to the main idea. We took the list of 24 different things that you could do to an experiment—not nearly all of them by the way—and tried a couple of them out on the prism setup.

Double it: Get a second prism and see if you can continue to separate the colors farther by lining up a second prism in the rainbow of the first.

Reduce it: Figure out a way to gather up the colors that have been produced and mix them back together to produce white light again.

Reverse it: Experiment with moving the flashlight and paper closer to the mirror and farther away. Draw a picture and be able to predict what happens to the size and clarity of the rainbow image.

Substitute it: You can also create a rainbow on a sunny day using a garden hose with a fine-spray nozzle attached. Set the nozzle adjustment so that a fine mist is produced and move the mist around in the sunshine until you see the rainbow. This works better if the sun is lower in the sky; late afternoon is best.

Hypothesis Work Sheet

Step Three (Expanded) • *Bend, Fold, Spindle Work Sheet*

This work sheet will give you an opportunity to work through the process of creating an original idea.

A. Write down the lab idea that you want to mangle.

_____

_____

_____

_____

B. List the possible variables you could change in the lab.

i. _____

ii. _____

iii. _____

iv. _____

v. _____

C. Take one variable listed in section B and apply one of the 24 changes listed below to it. Write that change down and state your new lab idea in the space below. Do that with three more changes.

Heat it	Freeze it	Reverse it	Double it
Bend it	Invert it	Poison it	Dehydrate it
Drown it	Stretch it	Fold it	Ignite it
Split it	Irradiate it	Oxidize it	Reduce it
Chill it	Speed it up	Color it	Grease it
Expand it	Substitute it	Remove it	Slow it down

i. _____

_____

_____

_____

ii. _____

_____

_____

_____

iii. _____

_____

_____

_____

iv. _____

STRETCHING!

_____

_____

_____

Step Four • Create an Original Idea— Your Hypothesis
Your hypothesis should be stated as an opinion. You've done the basic experiment, you've made observations, you're not stupid. Put two and two together and make a PREDICTION. Be sure that you are experimenting with just a single variable.

A. State your hypothesis in the space below. List the variable.
i. _____

_____

_____

_____

ii. Variable tested: _____

Sample Hypothesis Work Sheet

On the previous two pages is a work sheet that will help you develop your thoughts and a hypothesis. Here is sample of the finished product to help you understand how to use it.

A. Write down the lab idea that you want to mutilate.

A mirror is placed in a tub of water. A beam of light is focused through the water onto the mirror, producing a rainbow on the wall.

B. List the possible variables you could change in the lab.
 i. **Source of light**
 ii. **The liquid in the tub**
 iii. **The distance from flashlight to mirror**

C. Take one variable listed in section B and apply one of the 24 changes to it. Write that change down and state your new lab idea in the space below.

The shape of the beam of light can be controlled by making and placing cardboard filters over the end of the flashlight. Various shapes such as circles, squares, and slits will produce different quality rainbows.

D. State your hypothesis in the space below. List the variable. Be sure that when you write the hypothesis you are stating an idea and not asking a question.

Hypothesis: The narrower the beam of light the tighter, brighter, and more focused the reflected rainbow will appear.

Variable tested: **The opening on the filter**

Scientific Method
• Step 2 •
Gather Information

Gather Information

Read about your topic and find out what we already know. Check books, videos, the Internet, and movies, talk with experts in the field, and molest an encyclopedia or two. Gather as much information as you can before you begin planning your experiment.

In particular, there are several things that you will want to pay special attention to and that should accompany any good science fair project.

A. Major Scientific Concepts

Be sure that you research and explain the main idea(s) that is / are driving your experiment. It may be a law of physics or chemical rule or an explanation of an aspect of plant physiology.

B. Scientific Words

As you use scientific terms in your paper, you should also define them in the margins of the paper or in a glossary at the end of the report. You cannot assume that everyone knows about geothermal energy transmutation in sulfur-loving bacterium. Be prepared to define some new terms for them. . . and scrub your hands really well when you are done if that is your project.

C. Historical Perspective

When did we first learn about this idea, and who is responsible for getting us this far? You need to give a historical perspective with names, dates, countries, awards, and other recognition.

Building a Research Foundation

1. This sheet is designed to help you organize your thoughts and give you some ideas on where to look for information on your topic. When you prepare your lab report, you will want to include the background information outlined below.

    A. *Major Scientific Concepts (Two is plenty.)*

        i. _____

_____

_____

_____

        ii. _____

_____

_____

_____

    B. *Scientific Words (No more than 10)*

        i. _____

        ii. _____

        iii. _____

        iv. _____

        v. _____

        vi. _____

        vii. _____

        viii. _____

        ix. _____

        x. _____

    C. *Historical Perspective*
        Add this as you find it.

2. There are several sources of information that are available to help you fill in the details from the previous page.

A. *Contemporary Print Resources*
    (Magazines, Newspapers, Journals)

    i. _____
    ii. _____
    iii. _____
    iv. _____
    v. _____
    vi. _____

B. *Other Print Resources*
    (Books, Encyclopedias, Dictionaries, Textbooks)

    i. _____
    ii. _____
    iii. _____
    iv. _____
    v. _____
    vi. _____

C. *Celluloid Resources*
    (Films, Filmstrips, Videos)

    i. _____
    ii. _____
    iii. _____
    iv. _____
    v. _____
    vi. _____

D. *Electronic Resources:*
   (Internet Website Addresses, DVDs, MP3s)

   i. _____

   ii. _____

   iii. _____

   iv. _____

   v. _____

   vi. _____

   vii. _____

   viii. _____

   ix. _____

   x. _____

E. *Human Resources*
   (Scientists, Engineers, Professionals, Professors, Teachers)

   i. _____

   ii. _____

   iii. _____

   iv. _____

   v. _____

   vi. _____

You may want to keep a record of all of your research and add it to the back of the report as an Appendix. Some teachers who are into volume think this is really cool. Others, like myself, find it a pain in the tuchus. No matter what you do, be sure to keep an accurate record of where you find data. If you quote from a report word for word, be sure to give proper credit with either a footnote or parenthetical reference, this is very important for credibility and accuracy. This is will keep you out of trouble with plagiarism (copying without giving credit).

Scientific Method
• Step 3 •
Design Your Experiment

Acquire Your Lab Materials

The purpose of this section is to help you plan your experiment. You'll make a map of where you are going, how you want to get there, and what you will take along.

List the materials you will need to complete your experiment in the table below. Be sure to list multiples if you will need more than one item. Many science materials double as household items in their spare time. Check around the house before you buy anything from a science supply company or hardware store. For your convenience, we have listed some suppliers on page 19 of this book.

Material	Qty.	Source	$
1.			
2.			
3.			
4.			
5.			
6.			
7.			
8.			
9.			
10.			
11.			
12.			

Total $_____

Outline Your Experiment

This sheet is designed to help you outline your experiment. If you need more space, make a copy of this page to finish your outline. When you are done with this sheet, review it with an adult, make any necessary changes, review safety concerns on the next page, prepare your data tables, gather your equipment, and start to experiment.

In the space below, list what you are going to do in the order you are going to do it.

i. _____

_____

_____

ii. _____

_____

_____

_____

iii. _____

_____

_____

_____

iv. _____

_____

_____

_____

v. _____

_____

_____

_____

Evaluate Safety Concerns

We have included an overall safety section in the front of this book on pages 16–18, but there are some very specific questions you need to ask, and prepare for, depending on the needs of your experiment. If you find that you need to prepare for any of these safety concerns, place a check mark next to the letter.

_____ *A. Goggles & Eyewash Station*
If you are mixing chemicals or working with materials that might splinter or produce flying objects, goggles and an eyewash station or sink with running water should be available.

_____ *B. Ventilation*
If you are mixing chemicals that could produce fire, smoke, fumes, or obnoxious odors, you will need to use a vented hood or go outside and perform the experiment in the fresh air.

_____ *C. Fire Blanket or Fire Extinguisher*
If you are working with potentially combustible chemicals or electricity, a fire blanket and extinguisher nearby are a must.

_____ *D. Chemical Disposal*
If your experiment produces a poisonous chemical or there are chemical-filled tissues (as in dissected animals), you may need to make arrangements to dispose of the by-products from your lab.

_____ *E. Electricity*
If you are working with materials and developing an idea that uses electricity, make sure that the wires are in good repair, that the electrical demand does not exceed the capacity of the supply, and that your work area is grounded.

_____ *F. Emergency Phone Numbers*
Look up and record the following phone numbers for the Fire Department: _____ , Poison Control: _____ , and Hospital: _____ . Post them in an easy-to-find location.

Prepare Data Tables

Finally, you will want to prepare your data tables and have them ready to go before you start your experiment. Each data table should be easy to understand and easy for you to use.

A good data table has a **title** that describes the information being collected, and it identifies the **variable** and the **unit** being collected on each data line. The variable is *what* you are measuring and the unit is *how* you are measuring it. They are usually written like this:

Variable (unit), or to give you some examples:

Time (seconds)
Distance (meters)
Electricity (volts)

An example of a well-prepared data table looks like the sample below. We've cut the data table into thirds because the book is too small to display the whole line.

Determining the Boiling Point of Compound X_1

Time (min.)	0	1	2	3	4	5	6
Temp. (ºC)							

Time (min.)	7	8	9	10	11	12	13
Temp. (ºC)							

Time (min.)	14	15	16	17	18	19	20
Temp. (ºC)							

Scientific Method
• Step 4 •
Conduct the Experiment

Lab Time

It's time to get going. You've generated a hypothesis, collected the materials, written out the procedure, checked the safety issues, and prepared your data tables. Fire it up. Here's the short list of things to remember as you experiment.

_____ *A. Follow the Procedure, Record Any Changes*

Follow your own directions specifically as you wrote them. If you find the need to change the procedure once you are into the experiment, that's fine; it's part of the process. Make sure to keep detailed records of the changes. When you repeat the experiment a second or third time, follow the new directions exactly.

_____ *B. Observe Safety Rules*

It's easier to complete the lab activity if you are in the lab rather than the emergency room.

_____ *C. Record Data Immediately*

Collect temperatures, distances, voltages, revolutions, and any other variables and immediately record them into your data table. Do not think you will be able to remember them and fill everything in after the lab is completed.

_____ *D. Repeat the Experiment Several Times*

The more data that you collect, the better. It will give you a larger data base and your averages are more meaningful. As you do multiple experiments, be sure to identify each data set by date and time so you can separate them out.

_____ *E. Prepare for Extended Experiments*

Some experiments require days or weeks to complete, particularly those with plants and animals or the growing of crystals. Prepare a safe place for your materials so your experiment can continue undisturbed while you collect the data. Be sure you've allowed enough time for your due date.

Scientific Method
• Step 5 •
Collect and Display Data

Types of Graphs

This section will give you some ideas on how you can display the information you are going to collect as a graph. A graph is simply a picture of the data that you gathered portrayed in a manner that is quick and easy to reference. There are four kinds of graphs described on the next two pages. If you find you need a leg up in the graphing department, we have a book in the series called *Data Tables & Graphing*. It will guide you through the process.

Line and Bar Graphs

These are the most common kinds of graphs. The most consistent variable is plotted on the "x", or horizontal, axis and the more temperamental variable is plotted along the "y", or vertical, axis. Each data point on a line graph is recorded as a dot on the graph and then all of the dots are connected to form a picture of the data. A bar graph starts on the horizontal axis and moves up to the data line.

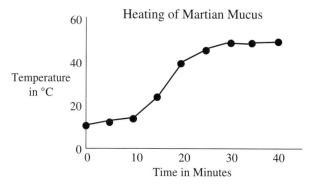

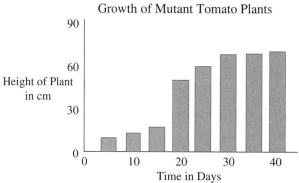

Best Fit Graphs

A best fit graph was created to show averages or trends rather than specific data points. The data that has been collected is plotted on a graph just as on a line graph, but instead of drawing a line from point to point to point, which sometimes is impossible anyway, you just free hand a line that hits "most of the data."

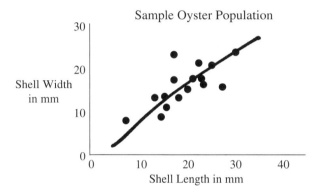

Pie Graphs

Pie graphs are used to show relationships between different groups. All of the data is totaled up and a percentage is determined for each group. The pie is then divided to show the relationship of one group to another.

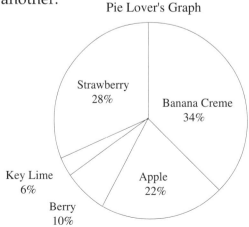

Other Kinds of Data

1. Written Notes & Observations

This is the age-old technique used by all scientists. Record your observations in a lab book. Written notes can be made quickly as the experiment is proceeding, and they can then be expounded upon later. Quite often notes made in the heat of an experiment are revisited during the evaluation portion of the process, and they can shed valuable light on how or why the experiment went the way it did.

2. Drawings

Quick sketches as well as fully developed drawings can be used as a way to report data for a science experiment. Be sure to title each drawing and, if possible, label what it is that you are looking at. Drawings that are actual size are best.

3. Photographs, Videotapes, and Audiotapes

Usually better than drawings, quicker, and more accurate, but you do have the added expense and time of developing the film. However, they can often capture images and details that are not usually seen by the naked eye.

4. The Experiment Itself

Some of the best data you can collect and present is the actual experiment itself. Nothing will speak more effectively for you than the plants you grew, the specimens you collected, or that big pile of tissue that was an armadillo you peeled from the tread of an 18-wheeler.

Scientific Method
· Step 6 ·
Present Your Ideas

Oral Report Checklist

It is entirely possible that you will be asked to make an oral presentation to your classmates. This will give you an opportunity to explain what you did and how you did it. Quite often this presentation is part of your overall score, so if you do well, it will enhance your chances for one of the bigger awards.

To prepare for your oral report, your science fair presentation should include the following components:

Physical Display

_____a.   freestanding display board
                hypothesis
                data tables, graphs, photos, etc.
                abstract (short summary)
_____b.   actual lab setup (equipment)

Oral Report

_____a.   hypothesis or question
_____b.   background information
                concepts
                word definitions
                history or scientists
_____c.   experimental procedure
_____d.   data collected
                data tables
                graphs
                photos or drawings
_____e.   conclusions and findings
_____f.   ask for questions

Set the display board up next to you on the table. Transfer the essential information to index cards. Use the index cards for reference, but do not read from them. Speak in a clear voice, hold your head up, and make eye contact with your peers. Ask if there are any questions before you finish and sit down.

Written Report Checklist

Next up is the written report, also called your lab write-up. After you compile or sort the data you have collected during the experiment and evaluate the results, you will be able to come to a conclusion about your hypothesis. Remember, disproving an idea is as valuable as proving it.

This sheet is designed to help you write up your science fair project and present your data in an organized manner. This is a final checklist for you.

To prepare your write-up, your science fair report should include the following components:

```
_____ a.    binder
_____ b.    cover page, title, & your name
_____ c.    abstract (one paragraph summary)
_____ d.    table of contents with page numbers
_____ e.    hypothesis or question
_____ f.    background information
                    concepts
                    word definitions
                    history or scientists
_____ g.    list of materials used
_____ h.    experimental procedure
                    written description
                    photo or drawing of setup
_____ i.    data collected
                    data tables
                    graphs
                    photos or drawings
_____ j.    conclusions and findings
_____ k.    glossary of terms
_____ l.    references
```

Display Checklist

2. Prepare your display to accompany the report. A good display should include the following:

Freestanding Display

_____	a.	freestanding cardboard back
_____	b.	title of experiment
_____	c.	your name
_____	d.	hypothesis
_____	e.	findings of the experiment
_____	f.	photo or illustrations of equipment
_____	g.	data tables or graphs

Additional Display Items

_____	h.	a copy of the write-up
_____	i.	actual lab equipment setup

Glossary,
Index,
and
More Ideas

Glossary

Bimetallic Strips
A tool composed of two different metal strips attached side by side. When the combined strip is heated in a hot flame, the metals expand at different rates causing the strip to bend. When the curved strip cools, it slowly straightens out and takes its original shape.

Calorie
Contrary to popular belief, not some mysterious ingredient in food that seeks out thighs, chins, and lower bellies, a calorie is the unit used to measure the amount of heat energy an object possesses. One calorie of heat will raise the temperature of one milliliter of water 1 degree Celsius.

Carbon Dioxide
A common gas that is critical to life here on Earth. We exhale carbon dioxide, and plants absorb it and convert it to complex carbohydrates. In the study of heat it is usually used in the solid form, which is not only very cold but also produces tons of cool effects.

Condensation Point
The temperature where gases cool down enough to condense and change to liquids.

Conduction
The method that heat uses to move through solid objects. When the heat is absorbed by the solid atoms in one area, they start to vibrate faster and faster, bumping the atoms next to them, bumping the atoms next to them, bumping the atoms next to them, and you get the idea. It is like a pile of dominos falling over. The heat is passed from atom to atom.

Convection Chimney
A tool used to demonstrate the presence of convection currents. It consists of two chimneys, side by side, inserted in the top of a box. A candle is placed under one chimney and a stick of incense is place over the other chimney. As the air inside the first chimney is heated, a convection current is set up inside the box, traced by the incense.

Convection Current

The upward movement of warm gases or liquids relative to cooler surrounding gases or liquids. These warmer currents eventually cool and descend. This cyclical movement is called a convection current and is generally the term used to describe how heat moves through liquids and gases.

Curie Point

The temperature at which an iron wire loses its magnetic abilities. The general thinking is that iron atoms will be attracted to a magnet. However, if those iron atoms are being heated and they lose their ability to stay lined up or even be attracted to a magnetic field because they are blipping around too much, that is called the Curie point.

Diffusion

Being completely confused about a number of different things. No, just kidding. The dispersal of a concentrated gas or liquid. If you open a plastic container of stinky eggs, that smell will go from being trapped inside the container to spreading out through the entire room. That is diffusion of a very unpleasant nature. When you place a tea bag in a cup of hot water, the chemicals in the tea diffuse throughout the water and become less dense.

Drinking Bird

A novelty toy that bobs back and forth when water on the felt-covered head evaporates causing the movement of liquids inside the glass body of the bird to fall out of equilibrium.

Electromagnetic Radiation

Energy that originates at the Sun and is composed of many of the known kinds of energy including visible light, cosmic rays, infrared radiation, ultraviolet radiation, radio wave, television waves, and so forth.

Endothermic Reaction

An endothermic reaction refers to a reaction between two chemicals where heat is absorbed from the environment. In this case the two chemicals feel cool to the touch.

Glossary

Exothermic Reactions

An exothermic reaction refers to a reaction between two chemicals where heat is produced by the reaction. In this case the two chemicals feel hot to the touch, that is if it has not already burst into flames.

Evaporation

The transition that takes place when a liquid changes to a gas.

Freezing Point

The temperature at which a liquid becomes solid. This is different for every substance and is used as an identifying characteristic.

Friction

The amount of resistant contact between two surfaces.

Hand Boiler

A novelty item that consists of two partially evacuated spheres connected by a narrow tube. The liquid inside the sphere has a low boiling point due to the reduced pressure inside the glass, so all it takes is the heat from the palm of your hand to cause the liquid to boil.

Heat Capacity

The measure of the ability of a material to hold heat—kind of like a sponge. The more heat—defined as calories—that something can hold, the greater its heat capacity. As a general rule this ability is also closely aligned with the density of the material—the more dense the material the greater the heat capacity.

Ice Bath

A container full of ice, usually a beaker or tub, that is used to cool containers rapidly.

Infrared Heat

This is the warmth of the sun that you feel when you run around outside in your nothin's. It is a wavelength that is just a little bit longer than visible light and can be experienced directly by placing your hand under a heating lamp at a restaurant.

Insulation

Any material that prevents or inhibits the movement of heat.

Kindling Point

The temperature where a material catches on fire or combusts.

Kinetic Heat

Heat that is produced by the movement of two objects rubbing on, passing over, or moving relative to one another. Rub your hands together and the movement of the skin of one hand against the skin of the other hand produces heat. Drop a rock out of the Space Shuttle, and it will burn up due to the friction of the air molecules against the stone. Bend a wire back and forth and the atoms inside the wire produce heat when they rub against one another—heat produced by motion.

Melting Point

The temperature where a solid becomes a liquid.

Nichrome Wire

A metal wire made out of a combination of nickel and chromium. It has a very high resistance, so when electricity flows through it, it becomes very hot, very easily. Most of the wire found in hair dryers, toaster, small ovens, and heating dishes are made using nichrome wire.

Nitinol Wire

Another metal-alloy wire consisting of nichrome—big surprise there—and titanium. The cool thing about this wire is that instead of expanding when it is heated, like most metals, it contracts. This characteristic allows you to bend, mold, twist, and mangle the wire into any shape that you want and it will return to its original shape when heated.

Glossary

Radiometer

A tool used to measure radiant energy that consists of a needle with a lightweight, four-sided vane that has one black side and the other side silvered. When radiant energy hits the vanes, the infrared spectrum is absorbed by the black side of the vanes and released into a partial vacuum. The release produces a small push that causes the vane to move.

Ring and Ball

An instructional tool composed of two instruments. A metal ring on the end of a long, thick wire and a solid, metal ball on the end of a long, thick wire. When both elements are at room temperature, the ball will fit nicely through the ring. When the ball is heated, it expands—as metal does—to the point where it will no longer fit through the ring.

Solar Hot Air Balloon

A large piece of black plastic that is inflated, tied off, and placed in direct sunlight. As the infrared radiation of the sun strikes and heats the gases trapped inside the balloon, they expand and the balloon becomes less dense relative to the surrounding air. As the balloon becomes lighter and lighter, the balloon starts to float.

Specific Heat

The amount of heat a given mass of material can hold. Measured in calories and determined by the increase in temperature of one gram of water, the specific heat varies from material to material and can be used as an identifying characteristic. Among metals the more dense the metal is the greater the specific heat.

Spontaneous Combustion

Just what it sounds like. Something that appears to burst into flames and catch on fire for no apparent reason. In chemistry the reason is that the energy stored in the molecular bonds is sufficient enough to start a fire once they are released.

Sublimation

The process of changing directly from a solid to a gas or a gas to a solid without taking time to become a liquid.

Temperature

The average amount of heat in a substance — completely and without question independent of the mass of that object.

Temperature Gradient

A gradient or gradual change, up or down, in temperature. Hold the end of a spoon in a very hot cup of hot chocolate, and as the spoon acquires more and more kinetic energy from the liquid, the spoon will get hotter and hotter.

Thermodynamics

The study of heat.

Thermometers

A tool used to measure the average amount of heat found in a substance. Invented over five centuries ago, common thermometers are based on and use three scales: Fahrenheit, Celsius, and Kelvin.

Transfer of Heat

The movement of heat from one object to another. Movement from solid to solid is called conduction, liquids and gases use convection, and gases and the vacuum of space incorporate radiation.

Vapor

Water that has reached its evaporation point and disappeared into the air.

Index

Index

Notes

Notes

Notes

Notes

Notes

Notes

Notes

Notes

Notes

Notes

More Science Books

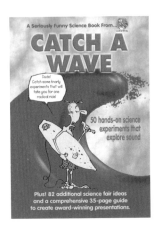

Catch a Wave
50 hands-on lab activities that sound off on the topic of noise, vibration, waves, the Doppler effect, and associated ideas.

Gravity Works
50 hands-on lab activities from the world of things that fly. Air, air pressure, Bernoulli's law, and all things that fly, float, or glide are explored.

Newton Take 3
50 hands-on lab activities that explore the world of mechanics, forces, gravity, and Newton's three laws of motion.

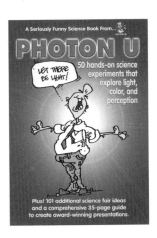

Photon U
50 hands-on lab activities from the world of light. Starts with the basic colors of the rainbow and works you way up to polarizing filters and UV light.

Electron Herding 101
50 hands-on lab activities that introduce static electricity, circuit electricity, and include a number of fun and very easy-to-build projects.

Opposites Attract
50 hands-on lab activities that delve into the world of natural and man-made magnets as well as the characteristics of magnetic attraction.

Thermodynamic Thrills • Winholtz, Cramer, Twyman, & Hixson